Tarot Dynamics Unleashed

By

Anna Burroughs Cook

Published by:
Kima Global Publishers
Kima Global House
50, Clovelly Road,
Clovelly
7975
South Africa

ISBN 978-1-920533-07-6

First Edition November 2011

Websites:

Publisher: http://www.kimaglobal.co.za

Author: http://www.tarotdynamics.com

ACKNOWLEDGEMENTS

It's been three years since the publication of my original "Tarot Dynamics." So this time, in addition to acknowledging my won- derful husband, plus our dogs Suzie Q, Buddy and Cagney, as well as my oldest friends and supporters, I'd also like to thank some new friends I've made along the way whose unflagging support and insight has also proved invaluable to me. People like Bonnie Cehovet, renowned Tarot reviewer and author of her wonderful book "Tarot Birth Cards and You", as well as Solandia web-hostess of the incomparable "Aeclectic Tarot." Mary Nale, Vice President of the Tarot Guild. Colin McQuillan "The Tarot Visionary." Mary Brown – aka Tarot Dactyl, of the Tarot Guild. Zanna Starr, author of that fabulous Tarot Blog, Tarot Notes-Major and Minor." Kate Chapman, co-author of "Beyond the Celtic Cross" and web-hostess for the inspirational "Tarot Elements." Not to mention, Koneta Bailey,Joanne Matthews, Stella Luna and Theresa Reed-"The Tarot Lady." Plus each and every on-line member of my "Tarot Dynamics Group" on Face Book, as well as Melinda Carver - an incredible psychic and personal friend. Last but not least, two people who are very close to my heart, the pioneering and insightful Victoria Evangelina Belyavskaya from Uzbekistan and MY astrologer the esteemed Marie McGovern, past president of the Akron Ohio, Astrological Society, who graciously took the time to proof-read my Astrological conclusions in "Tarot Dynamics Unleashed." Also my publishers and good friends Robin Beck and the celebrated author Nadine May, from Kima Global Publishing, for giving a still "new author" , yet another opportunity to be heard. Thank-You all for everything you've done.

August 8, 2011 Anna Burroughs Cook

DEDICATION

This book is dedicated to the memory of Eleanor Mannochio and Ella Pringle

May you have the foresight to know where you're going,
The hindsight to know where you've been,
And the insight to know where you are.

Irish Proverb

FOREWORD

Hello and welcome to "Tarot Dynamics Unleashed." To those of you who are already familiar with "Tarot Dynamics" I'd like to say, "Welcome Back," and rest assured that your old favorites (such as our Do's and Don'ts, Tarot card Definitions, and Basic Tarot spread information[1]) are all still here, though many now contain additional detail. However they're all traveling with a great deal of exciting all new and in-depth, Tarot information that will enable your Tarot cards to take your intuition farther than you ever dreamed via chapters that explain Tarot and Numerology, as well as Fallen Cards[2] while Chapter 10 (Tarot Dynamics and the Moon in Astrology) will clearly and finally reveal the first missing-link between the Tarot and Astrology.

So should you be new to the Tarot, or the Tarot Dynamics method, you'll find that the examples, definitions and information in "Tarot Dynamics Unleashed" is as easy for the beginner or intermediate Tarot student to understand, as it is to follow, while more adept readers will find it easier than ever to blend the old with the new. Just like "Tarot Dynamics", the information in Tarot Dynamics Unleashed" is still able to accommodate the seventy-eight card Tarot Deck of your choice!

Anna Burroughs Cook

---

[1] One-Card, Three-Card, Celtic Cross- now called Tarot Dynamics in Action and the Horoscope Spread.
[2] Entitled: What Falls To The Floor Comes To The Door."

TABLE OF CONTENTS

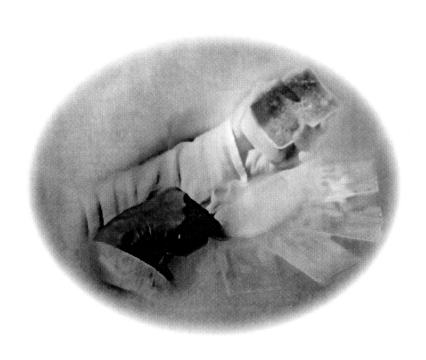

INTRODUCTION

There are some things that we do not believe unless we understand them, and some things we do not understand unless we believe them.-

Saint Augustin

The accuracy of any forecast from the stock market, to the weather, or the future success of a single individual relies upon the sensitivity and skill of the interpreter. The art of reading the Tarot has been a respected (if somewhat mysterious) form of divination for hundreds of years. There have been many debates about the Tarot's specific origins but its roots can be traced back to one of the original versions found in the Kabbalah, a book of Hebrew traditions and Gnostic knowledge. This book is intended to be a study guide to help you master the Tarot and develop your own technique for interpreting the cards.

DO'S and DON'TS

DO memorize the characteristics for the five Tarot suits.

DO develop your own keywords. How? After having read this book and absorbed its guidelines, sit down with a pen and paper and study the picture of each card in your deck. Write down a keyword that describes what you "feel" when you see that card, anger, enlightenment, success, worry, travel, promotion etc. Use **your** keywords. Whether or not your definition for a particular card agrees with anyone else's is NOT important as long as the information you provide is correct.

DO be as creative as you wish. Devising your own Tarot spread can be fun. However, the longer you work with the Tarot, the sooner you'll realize that the accuracy of your reading depends strictly upon your ability to correctly interpret the cards NOT the Tarot spread.

DO not be surprised, once you've learned to relax, if you discover that doing a reading for someone else is much easier than trying to read a Tarot spread for yourself!

DO you have to memorize too much? Not if you don't want to.

Memorizing the five keywords for each of the five suits will suffice if you are more curious than serious about learning the Tarot and uninterested in reading any Tarot decks except the one featured in this book.

DON'T read the cards for yourself unless you're relaxed and in control of your emotions. Otherwise, the cards are more likely to echo your anxiety, which won't help matters.

DON'T do a full reading of the cards for yourself or anyone else too often. I won't read for a client more often than every three to six months. Give matters time to develop. Remember too, that the greater the affection between you and the person you're reading, the harder it is to remain as open and objective as you should be.

DON'T read the cards for other people who are upset. Postpone their reading until they've calmed down. Otherwise, the cards will simply echo their anxiety and your reading will prove inaccurate.

DON'T read the cards for anyone who intimidates you. If your information is inaccurate, they'll never let you forget it. If you're correct, they'll chalk your success up to luck.

DON'T expect the reading you conduct today to solve any and every issue that could possibly impact the Seekers life tomorrow or next week. Should you see a change of plans or direction appearing on their horizon, but cannot determine the cause, simply suggest that the Seeker keep their schedule as flexible as possible in the near future to better accommodate incoming changes from more than one matter, at work, home and possibly both.

ABOUT TAROT DECKS

There are over a thousand different Tarot decks to choose from today, - and there's sure to be more tomorrow, any and all of which, can serve as a means to enhance or unleash your personal intuition.

While many Tarot decks contain seventy-eight (78) cards designed to portray the inner-vision that each author and/ or artist believes will strengthen the readers personal connection to the Tarot and their higher or inner-self, some can contain eighty (80) or more cards, while others can number from as little as twenty-one (21) to sixty-four cards, allegedly designed to assist the reader in discovering and understanding their purpose in life and/or their spiritual connection to nature as well as one another.

However, there are also some Tarot decks which feature only the Major Arcana, and others whose suit names were simply designed to compliment the artists theme.

Nonetheless, the first category and suit in most Tarot Decks is called the Major Arcana, while the second category is called the Minor Arcana, which is comprised of four more suits, that are best known as known as the Wands, Cups, Swords and Pentacles.

THE RIDER-WAITE-SMITH (RWS) TAROT FORMAT

Since 1909 the best-known Tarot decks are those that contain seventy-eight Tarot cards as well as a small white instruction booklet and subscribe to the Rider-Waite-Smith (RWS) Tarot format. The original Rider-Waite Tarot deck, designed for Arthur Edward-Waite by the artist, Pamela Colman Smith was the first seventy-eight card Tarot deck to feature imagery on the Pips (numbered cards) Before the release of Miss Smiths' designs only the Major Arcana and Court Cards (or trumps) contained pictures. Each Subject Card (or pip) featured the designated number of symbols floating in the air. You can see the difference in the example below, featuring Card 46 the Six of Cups from the Rider-Waite Tarot Deck by Lo Scarabeo on the left and Card 46 the Six of Cups on the right from a another Tarot Deck by Lo Scarabeo featuring 3 Cups on each side.

The more comfortable you are ,with whatever key words and definitions you apply to your favorite deck of tarot cards, the easier and more intuitively you can conduct an accurate (not cookie-cutter) reading when reading from any Tarot Deck whose imagery and colors appeal to you.

To clarify that statement, example two (below) features Card 62 the Eight of Swords from Lo Scarabeos Rider-Waite Tarot Deck (on the left) and The Eight of Swords from Lo Scarabeos Universal Goddess Tarot Deck (on the right)

The only similarity between these cards is the name and number of the Suit—Eight of Swords. Look closely. If you're a beginner you may wish to read the definition found in Chapter 5.

Should you be more advanced however, feel free to apply whatever definition you associate with the Eight of Swords, because chances are, your definition will be appropriate for both cards. If so, that's well and good. However, if the definition that you're accustomed to, doesn't seem to express everything that "you feel" when you look at each card - that's even better, and perfectly natural! Here's why.

Working with the Tarot tends to enhance your awareness and psychic sensitivity, via color and form, and each Tarot deck has something different to offer. Whether or not your definition for a particular Tarot card always agrees with what you first learned is not important as long as the information you provide is accurate.

Once you've mastered the basics of your first Tarot deck, reading different decks from time to time, is also the best way to keep your perspective fresh and your intuition sharp!

SELECTING THE TAROT DECKS THAT ARE BESTFOR YOU

I invite clients who come to my office to select the Tarot Deck of their choice for me to read from. I also encourage students# to purchase at least two Tarot decks. Here's why. It's very important that you become familiar with one Tarot deck before you begin working with others. Although you may feel more comfortable learning the Tarot from the featured deck in this study guide, it may be best for honing your reading technique than fully unleashing your intuition.

When I began teaching the Tarot, it was customary that students learn the Tarot from identical decks. Although each student performed well with the prescribed deck, most, longed to work with different decks whose colors and illustrations held more appeal for them. So, shortly before graduation, I suggested they purchase whatever deck they wished to use for their last night in class. The results were amazing! Students, who had done well, became outstanding and students who had been struggling suddenly became superstars! After that episode, I always suggested that my students choose two decks from the beginning, at least one of which should be the RWS or an RWS

clone, as they are the most "reader-friendly" and the most frequently used in Tarot classes, books and seminars.

Last but not least, the more familiar you become with only one Tarot Deck, the easier it is to overlook what appears to be less significant, and underestimate certain challenges that can prove to be more than you bargained for!

People tend to choose Tarot decks whose colors and illustrations match their subconscious (rather than conscious) mood. People with more pressing concerns often choose colors that are softer-more soothing; whereas people with greater confidence, daring or optimism are likely to choose more striking colors.

The less active you (or the seekers) life (whether for better or worse) the more likely you are to read from the same Tarot deck time after time, whereas the more active or colorful your situation the more likely you are to begin purchasing and reading from a wider variety of Tarot decks.

Should you (or the seeker) habitually choose a different deck for each reading, but suddenly begin to favor one particular deck you may also be experiencing greater stability or peace of mind in your life. Should you consistently read from the same deck, but suddenly begin reading from different Tarot decks, subconsciously, if not consciously you may be wrestling with an important decision or preparing to accommodate a change that you can sense--but not yet see on your horizon.

"WORKING" TAROT DECKS AND PERSONAL TAROT DECKS

The term, "working" Tarot Decks refers to those one or two Tarot decks that you can always count on to tell you what you need to know. For instance, each Tarot deck that my clients choose from is one of my "working decks." For whatever reason, their simple imagery and basic colors are in synch with my intuition, enabling me to see more of what my clients need to know, more quickly. Each of them is a RWS clone. Although I do enjoy the more flamboyant or artistic Tarot decks, their breathtaking imagery fuels my imagination more than my intuition. That is why they remain in my collection of "personal" Tarot Decks—the ones I use to read for myself when pondering or meditating upon a more general concern. Whenever I need more specific insight, I always turn to one of my "working" Tarot decks. Over time, you're certain to discover what your best "working" decks are, and don't be surprised if your best "working" decks are the least glamorous in your collection!

AFTER PURCHASING YOUR TAROT CARDS

Remove the cards from the box and cellophane wrapper. Shuffle the cards for a few moments making sure you mix them very well before returning them to the box. During the days before you use your cards for the first time, you may either sleep with the box of cards under your pillow or on your nightstand. If your home is your primary base of operations, keep the box of cards near you as you perform your daily routines. Feel free to shuffle them occasionally. This exercise allows you and your cards to become more familiar with one another. However, if you work outside the home, carry them in your purse, or in the case of a man, in a briefcase or lunch pail. After using your cards for the first time return them to the box and select a special spot to store them until the next time you use them. Some people prefer wrapping their cards in a piece of silk or purchasing a special box in which to store their Tarot cards.

INTUITION VERSUS IMAGINATION

Yes. Everyone IS psychic - to some degree. The reason why some people are more psychic (or intuitive) than others stems from the fact that everyone's psychic ability manifests itself at different times and in different ways. It all depends upon what type of circumstances or conditions are necessary to "trigger" your intuition. For instance, music is one of the most common intuitive triggers. People, who regularly listen to the radio, often know what song will play next. While some people are more attuned to sensing changes before they occur in their daily environment, other people -whether upon meeting someone new or entering a new atmosphere, sometimes feel a pleasant connection, or inexplicable uneasiness. Whereas some people work more naturally with their intuition all their life, others only exhibit an extraordinary clarity and accuracy, now and then - and usually when then they least expect it.

Although most Readers are as efficient as they are proficient at correctly identifying your personal *and* professional circumstances, it's not unusual for one Reader to be more attuned to certain aspects of your personal life than your professional life (or vice versa). However, listening to what each one has to say, *should* provide a more complete picture of when, how or why what went wrong or suddenly turned around for the better - which may be part of the reason why reputable "ghost busters" often employ more than one psychic. Genuine intuition is spontaneous.

In my experience, the most accurate predictions are those that people suddenly exclaim for no discernable reason, such as walking into work one day and simply "knowing" before your boss does, that they will soon be announcing a merger, cutbacks or promotions. While some people are always more sensitive to objects, such as coins, jewelry or even clothing (to name a few) others are not - until, one day upon touching something at a flea market they *immediately* "know" whether it was a gift, impulse purchase or an heirloom, and they either purchase it immediately, or put as much distance as possible between themselves and the object. Although some people may never again experience an episode like that, for others, it may become a regular feature.

EVERYONE automatically becomes more sensitive to (some degree to) the moods of whatever company they are keeping - or avoiding, at work and home, and this is especially true whenever you conduct a Tarot Card reading for anyone other than yourself. In most instances, the more comfortable you feel with the seeker, the easier you can identify with their goals, or disappointments as well as whatever strengths they need to obtain them. From there, it's a short hop to "imagining" that the seeker cannot fail to win their objective, and dispensing suggestions, advice and encouragement based upon how YOU would handle their situation. However, that's common sense, not intuition. Should the Seeker be as much like yourself as you *imagine*, perhaps your "prediction" will be correct. However, should they be in transition, and not yet at the point where you are, your prediction will be at best, delayed and, at worst completely derailed. The most likely reason for predictions such as this going askew stem from the fact that no matter how similar we may be to anyone else, in thought, belief and experience each person tends to process and digest whatever they are growing through a little differently - which takes some people longer than others.

Intuition is what enables you to state with certainty and accuracy how many children the seeker has, or the condition of their employer's health, or a friends marriage, even the condition of the Seeker's home or automobile, personal health or health of a loved one etc. - *before* the seeker asks, because whatever you truly "intuit" is what the seeker will most need to know - whether or not it was what they were concerned about. In moments like these, you'll also discover that your cards that will support your intuitive statements to complete what more the Seeker needs to know.

Although not every Seeker, will trigger your intuition, the more comfortable you become with your Tarot cards the more you can rely on their colors and figures to trigger your intuition in small ways that will make big differences in even the most ordinary reading, and prevent you from "filling in the gaps" with what you "hope" or "imagine" will be best for the Seeker.

READING THE TAROT

The Tarot is like anything else - the longer you work with it the more proficient you'll become. Reading the Tarot also has a tendency to open or expand your intuitive faculties. Yes, you're probably going to be nervous when you begin to read the Tarot. You know you best. It may be two weeks or six months before you feel confident enough to do a reading without referring to this manual or notes you've taken. When you do deliver your very first "solo" reading, don't be surprised if the harder you try recall each keyword, definition or placement title, the more you rely on your own intuition - because that's exactly as it should be!

READING THE TAROT FOR OTHER PEOPLE

Getting over *yourself* is the first step to reading the Tarot successfully. The greater your fear of saying the wrong thing, the more likely it is you will. By the same token -- the more you think you know, the more you're sure to learn. Until, and unless, you can detach yourself from your ego, worries, or self- doubt, you shouldn't attempt to read the Tarot. Why? Because whenever you do a reading for someone else all your sensitivity and awareness needs to be focused on the other person. Detaching yourself from your own concerns can be achieved more easily by developing and applying your own technique for personal relaxation before doing a reading. If you haven't yet discovered a personal relaxation technique, here's what I'd suggest: Sit quietly with your eyes closed or look out the window. Imagine that you are in your favorite setting, perhaps a cool forest, or a warm and sandy beach, even a flowering meadow—whatever makes you feel calm and happy. If you're feeling particularly anxious, scattered or unsettled you may also wish to light incense or a scented candle, listen to soft music, or perform some simple exercises. After the reading, take a moment or two to shuffle your cards before returning them to their case.

READING THE TAROT FOR PEOPLE
AT A DISTANCE

Doing a Tarot reading by phone has gained popularity in recent years. If you're the caller, the reader allegedly concentrates upon you, shuffles the cards and proceeds to tell you what you want to hear - which is generally quite different from what you need to know! I have several clients living out of state who call for telephone readings a few times each year. Yet, I would never dream of shuffling cards for them. They each have their own deck of Tarot cards which they shuffle before they call me. Doing this insures that their reading is uncontaminated by any outside influence. It also affords me a clear picture of what they need to know. Then we proceed to lay out the cards together while I record the session. When we're finished, I mail the CD to them for future reference. I suggest this technique for two reasons: First, it lends the reading a personal touch second it increases my accuracy.

READING YOUR OWN TAROT CARDS

Doing an accurate reading for yourself requires that you remain neutral and objective. Some people start each day by drawing and interpreting one Tarot card from their own deck, or selecting a one or three card reading from Tarot Web Site - similar to reading your daily horoscope in the newspaper. It's not often that I read my own Tarot cards, but when I do, I only employ the three-card spread (see Chapter Eight). Whenever I'm seriously in need of insight about a matter, I prefer to consult another Tarot reader. Why? Because, the more significant the situation, the harder it becomes NOT to interpret the definitions according to what I want to be true or fear the most. The same will be true for you.

Once, when I was very new to reading the Tarot, I had a client who appeared in a state of high anxiety. Shortly after I began to read, they began to get agitated. Upon reaching the conclusion, they were quite irritable. Since they were obviously displeased, I declined payment for my services. Nonetheless, I wanted to know how I had offended them. Upon voicing this question, the client haughtily replied that they too read the Tarot. In fact, they read their own cards EVERY day and not one thing I'd told them had appeared in their cards! I was quite surprised when a few weeks later they called again. This time they were upset because my reading proved accurate; they wanted to know if I had jinxed them. I reassured them that I certainly had not jinxed them and gently suggested that perhaps their own emotional strength and intensity had led them to misinterpret when they read for themselves. This story illustrates how reading for yourself can wind up an exercise in hearing what we want instead of what we need to know. Flooding yourself with more information than you can process, is another downside to reading your own cards too often.

YOUR TAROT-DYNAMIC DEFINITIONS

Tarot Dynamics has been formatted and designed to accompany the seventy-eight card Tarot Deck of YOUR choice. Simply place the matching Tarot Card from your Tarot deck over the illustrations to reinforce your learning experience!

Unlike other Tarot books, your "Tarot Dynamic" definitions have been crafted to assist you in unleashing your intuition. However, each definition contains two very important phrases that begin with: "The more encouraging the situation", or, "the more challenging the situation". These terms refer to reasons for conducting the reading. If for example, you or the person you're reading has discovered you're in line for a promotion or a new job—that's an "encouraging situation". Receiving good news or coming up with a fresh idea, or experiencing a "hunch" that tells you matters will soon be taking a turn for the better are also good examples of encouraging situations.

Consulting the cards will reveal more of what you need to know about your new hope or endeavor. By the same token, should you or the person you're reading discover you're in danger of being downsized on your job that's a "more challenging

situation". Yet, whether you're feeling less positive, or have recently received unsettling news, viewing your entire spread to see whether any particular suit or subject card (numbers two through ten) hold a majority can also tell you more of what you need to know concerning alternative options and avenues. Chapter 9 offers several examples to assist you.

A short section entitled For New Students, also accompanies each Tarot definition to simplify your learning process.

A HINT OF ROMANCE

The definition for each Court Card as well as the entire suit of Cups contains an additional subheading (entitled romantically) beginning with the phrase: "Should your spread contain a hint of romance". However, there are no hard and fast rules concerning what "a hint of romance" looks like in the Tarot. You see, whether at the beginning, the middle, or the end each romance and every romantic opportunity is as different as the couples that encounter them.

When the client asks, "Can I expect to meet my true love soon?" differentiating between opportunity and wishful thinking in the cards poses a real challenge. I have found it easier to resolve issues concerning romance, as well as romantic misunderstandings, by viewing the entire spread to determine which, if any, Court Cards happen to fall with, or near cards such as--The Lovers, the Empress, the Wheel of Fortune, The Star, or The Fool from Major Arcana as well as the Two, Three, Six, or Ten of Cups.

Here too, with a little time and practice as your intuition becomes stronger and more reliable you're sure to devise your own guidelines. Whether or not you or the person you're reading is involved in a relationship or hopes to find one, every now and then - you'll get a "feeling" from one or more particular cards or their alignment in your spread that alerts you to an impending change in their (or your) emotional situation, so follow your feelings!!!

DIFFERENTIATING BETWEEN A CHALLENGE AND AN INCONVIENENCE

No matter how rushed you are, a flat tire is more of an inconvenience than a challenge-- unless you lack the skill to change the tire yourself, or the means to purchase a new tire. Yet, by overcoming the challenge of learning to change your own tire, or by re-examining your financial situation, you confront the challenge, and that encourages you to become more resourceful and independent.

KEEPING MATTERS IN PERSPECTIVE

My favorite definition for the word challenge is; a matter or circumstance that requires our immediate attention. Interviewing for a better job is a personal challenge, but the possibility of landing that job overrides our anxiety concerning the interview. Whether or not it's expected, bad news from a doctor or dentist also presents a personal challenge, but the possibility of feeling better helps counteract any anxiety concerning the upcoming medical procedure. Loss of employment, or an unexpected reduction of income also presents a personal challenge, yet by taking the opportunity to develop marketable skills, or by simplifying our life, the initial challenge may prove to be a blessing in disguise.

FOR NEW STUDENTS

Since it's very important that you become familiar with ONE Tarot deck before you begin working with others, you may feel more comfortable learning the Tarot and unleashing your intuition by working with the Tarot deck featured in this study guide. However, since color and form ARE an integral part of unleashing your intuition, you are also free to work with any other seventy-eight card Tarot Deck whose colors and illustrations may hold more appeal for you. Although I would suggest starting with either the RWS Deck or a RWS clone, as their imagery is generally the most "reader-friendly", Tarot Dynamics has been formatted and designed to accompany the seventy-eight card Tarot Deck of YOUR choice. Simply place the matching Tarot Card from the Tarot deck of your choice over the illustrations to widen and reinforce your learning experience!

GETTING READY TO READ

Unlike other methods for learning the Tarot, whose keywords and key phrases, upright and reversed definitions often number in the hundreds, aside from the necessity of memorizing the name and number of each Tarot Card, the Tarot Dynamics method requires only nineteen key points of memorization. Let's begin now with the five easy keywords and simple definitions that best describe the functions for all five suits of the Tarot.

Suit: Major Arcana   **Function: Karma**
(cause and effect)

Karma is Tarot Dynamics chief keyword for describing the main function of each Major Arcana Card, and karma isn't always just about doing good deeds. It can be as simple as knowing when to leave well enough alone, or finally stepping up to the plate to confront a matter that we've been avoiding.

Suit: Wands   **Function: Change.**

New Growth. New Ways & Means to Blaze Your Own Trail.

Suit: Cups   **Function: Emotion.**

Your dreams and everything that gives meaning to your life.

Suit: Swords   **Function: Challenge.**

Swords engage your intellect, enabling you to put ideas into action, thoughts into words and bring order into chaos.

Suit: Pentacles   **Function: Ambition.**

Pentacles signify your desire for and opportunities to acquire, permanence and control of your emotional and economic concerns.

The fact that many people cannot read the Tarot without relying on someone else's definition has led many readers to assume that an accurate reading can only be achieved by following the individual definitions for each Tarot Deck.

Attempting to blend the various keywords and definitions is as distracting as it is time-consuming. This is also a major reason why many readers who collect numerous Tarot decks remain limited to reading only from the deck they used while learning. Situations like this have discouraged more than Tarot enthusiast causing them to believe they have failed when, in fact, the method from which they first learned to read the Tarot failed them by inhibiting, rather than, encouraging their intuitive self- reliance. That's why "Tarot Dynamics" has been designed to work with any and every 78-card Tarot deck, as well as to assist you in expanding your intuitive faculties while reading or mastering the Tarot - and our five keywords are the cornerstones that will enable you to do so.

The next 6 chapters will provide a comprehensive explanation of the five suits and 78 cards that comprise the Tarot. After reading chapters one through 6, memorizing the names and numbers of all seventy-eight cards is your next step in mastering the Tarot completely.

In 1980 after reading "Numerology and The Divine Triangle", (copyright 1979) by Faith Javane and Dusty Bunker, I immediately adopted their numbering sequence (1-78) for the Tarot. It's a tremendous advantage, whether you're learning the Tarot or teaching a Tarot class. Here's why. Everyone tends to identify more quickly and easily with the Major Arcana and the Court Cards than the Subject cards. In as little as one week (without looking at the illustrations) you can instantly visualize the correct Major Arcana or Court card as soon as you hear its' name! Yet, even the brightest students, often stumble a bit concerning the Subject cards - without looking at the individual illustrations.

Assigning a number to the name of each Tarot card enables you to visualize the correct card, without looking at the illustration, or having to stop and think, "oh my, is the Six of Pentacles, the figure holding the scales or standing by the bush?" Whether you hear or simply think the number 74, the correct image of the correct card will immediately spring to mind - accompanied by whatever mini-definition you are most comfortable with. Working with each suit in groups of five or ten worked well for me. Once you've memorized the names and numbers of one complete suit -- test yourself. Take a sheet of paper and write down the number for each card in that suit. Then, fill in the name of each card next to its assigned number and check your

notes or study-guide to see how right you are. Working with a study-buddy can also be fun.

Depending upon your schedule, it may take as little as three days or perhaps even a week, but once you can think of a random number, (for example) forty-three, and know that that number IS the Three of Cups you're on your way! Our list begins below.

MAJOR ARCANA

Card 1 the Magician

Card 2 the High Priestess

Card 3 the Empress

Card 4 the Emperor

Card 5 the Hierophant

Card 6 the Lovers

Card 7 the Chariot

Card 8 Strength

Card 9 the Hermit

Card 10 Fortunes Wheel

Card 11 Justice

MAJOR ARCANA

Card 12 the Hanged Man

Card 13 Death

Card 14 Temperance

Card 15 the Devil

Card 16 the Tower

Card 17 the Star

Card 18 the Moon

Card 19 the Sun

Card 20 Judgment

Card 21 The World

Card 22 the Fool

WANDS

Card 23 King of Wands

Card 24 Queen of Wands

Card 25 Knight of Wands

Card 26 Page of Wands

Card 27 Ace of Wands

Card 28 Two of Wands

Card 29 Three of Wands

WANDS

Card 30 Four of Wands

Card 31 Five Wands

Card 32 Six of Wands

Card 33 Seven of Wands

Card 34 Eight of Wands

Card 35 Nine of Wands

Card 36 Ten of Wands

CUPS

Card 37 King of Cups

Card 38 Queen of Cups

Card 39 Knight of Cups

Card 40 Page of Cups

Card 41 Ace of Cups

Card 42 Two of Cups

Card 43 Three of Cups

CUPS

Card 44 Four of Cups

Card 45 Five of Cups

Card 46 Six of Cups

Card 47 Seven of Cups

Card 48 Eight of Cups

Card 49 Nine of Cups

Card 50 Ten of Cups

SWORDS

Card 51 King of Swords

Card 52 Queen of Swords

Card 53 Knight of Swords

Card 54 Page of Swords

Card 55 Ace of Swords

Card 56 Two of Swords

Card 57 Three of Swords

SWORDS

Card 58 Four of Swords

Card 59 Five of Swords

Card 60 Six of Swords

Card 61 Seven of Swords

Card 62 Eight of Swords

Card 63 Nine of Swords

Card 64 Ten of Swords

PENTACLES

Card 65 King of Pentacles

Card 66 Queen of Pentacles

Card 67 Knight of Pentacles

Card 68 Page of Pentacles

Card 69 Ace of Pentacles

Card 70 Two of Pentacles

Card 71 Three of Pentacles

PENTACLES

Card 72 Four of Pentacles

Card 73 Five of Pentacles

Card 74 Six of Pentacles

Card 75 Seven of Pentacles

Card 76 Eight of Pentacles

Card 77 Nine of Pentacles

Card 78 Ten of Pentacles

The final step to deliver an effortless and accurate reading from any seventy-eight card Tarot Deck is to memorize one simple key phrase, for each of the five Court Cards and eight Subject cards from the Minor Arcana listed in Chapter 2. For example, "All Kings trigger or enhance your initiative", and "Subject card Number 3 represents Thinking and Networking". Please, don't hesitate to devise your own key phrase or keywords. For example, in Chapter 2 Subject Card Seven is said to represent relationships. However, you might choose "friends and lovers."

FAQ

Q. In my Tarot deck, the Magician, as well as the Ace of Wands, Ace of Cups, Ace of Swords and Ace of Pentacles are all labeled as a Number 1. Yet in Chapter 2 you mention that the only Number 1 in Tarot Dynamics is Card 1 the Magician. How do I reconcile this?

A. I can see how this might cause some confusion. For whatever reason, over the last fifteen to twenty years many Tarot Artists have proceeded to label the Magician as well as each Ace, with the Number One. In fact, one of my favorite "working" Tarot decks is also labeled in this fashion and lists the Fool as Card 0 instead of 22. So you have two choices. You can either do what I do and ignore the Number 1 on each Ace or you may wish to purchase one or more of the older Tarot Decks, like The Rider Waite Smith whose artists had the foresight to resist placing numerical limitations upon their artwork.

Q. Isn't it supposed to mean something when the picture on the Tarot card is upside down?

A. That depends upon the interpretation of your reader. Some readers apply the negative (or more challenging) definition to any Tarot card whose picture is reversed or upside down. Once you begin working with your cards it won't be long before you can recognize the difference between genuine challenges and temporary stumbling blocks or hesitation. In my experience it really doesn't matter, but I prefer to see all the cards right side up. Viewing them in this manner improves my range and accuracy.

Q. Why didn't the Tarot reader tell me as much information as my friend received?

A. There are two parts to this answer.

First: Some people hear more, while some hear less during their reading. Some people are going to be up against a wider variety of issues in the near future. Some are already on the path that's right for them, or their life is currently under better control or more organized.

Second: How often do you have your cards read? No matter how much you may like your reader, the better they get know you, the harder it is for them to retain their objectivity. It's in your best interest to space your readings at least three if not six months apart.

Q. I went to three different readers in 3 months and heard three different stories, how do I know who to believe?

A. Chances are that at least a little something from one or more of those readings will come to pass in time. Nonetheless, you're having your cards read too often! If you were comfortable with all three readers, I suggest that you schedule a return session in another three or four months with the reader who provided the most accurate information. If you weren't comfortable with any of those readers, consider shopping around for a reader who does suit you. That's very important. The more comfortable you and the reader feel with one another the more accurate and informative your session will be.

Q. All my cards were terrific - why didn't anything good happen?

A. Were you relaxed and simply concentrating on pleasant thoughts in general when you shuffled the cards? Or were you wishing really hard for something? Remember there really IS a connection between the cards and the person shuffling them that can't be explained. If you were wishing too hard that something would or wouldn't happen, those thoughts may have contaminated your cards. In other words, your mental intensity may have caused the cards to rearrange themselves in the deck according to what you wanted to see. If this was the case, the next time you meet with your reader relax when you shuffle the cards and don't try so hard. However, if you weren't wishing for anything in particular while you shuffled, did you work with your reading to encourage these brighter episodes to come to pass, or were you just waiting for all the goodness to fall from the sky?
y! Our list begins below.

ABOUT THE MAJOR ARCANA

Function: Headlines.

Keywords: Spiritual Karma.

All Major Arcana cards test, reward, and replenish your strength of character.

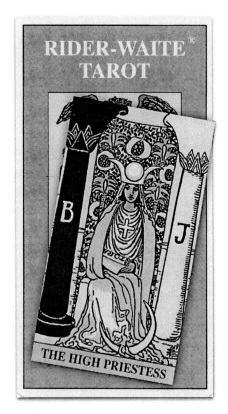

CHAPTER 1

The Major Arcana is the first of the five suits in the Tarot. It contains twenty-two (22) cards. When translated from Latin, the name Major Arcana means Big Secrets. Major Arcana cards grab your attention, like the headlines in a newspaper. Collectively, as well as individually, Major Arcana cards represent spiritual karma, which we are forever resolving, creating and/or re-creating, and *Tarot Dynamics* refers to Karma as cause and effect – as simple as knowing when to leave well enough alone, or finally stepping up to the plate to confront a matter that we've been avoiding. Each good or bad habit that we break ends some cycle of self-induced Karma, and every new goal we undertake sets a different chain of Karmic challenges in motion. While the individual definition for each card suggest the reason, the method through which Karma will be fulfilled, most often corresponds to one, very simple, very human, personal strength or weakness.

While Major Arcana Cards 1-10[1] tend to represent something you have earned through your recent behavior and actions, the tests, rewards, and situations, indicated by Major Arcana Cards 11–22[2] the Fool, often have a stronger effect upon your long-range goals, or destiny.

For example: you are the top salesperson in your shop. Yesterday Card 3 the Empress appeared in your reading, so you're anticipating a treat, and why not? After all,

---

[1] Major Arcana Cards 1-10, are the Magician through Fortunes Wheel.
[2] Major Arcana Cards 11-22 are Justice through the Fool.

"networking", (the chief keyword for Card 3) is your specialty, and "optimism", (Card 3's personal strength) is your trademark. Tomorrow, not caring care to deal with a new customer, who doesn't appear to be of value, you encourage an inexperienced co-worker to wait upon them. Next week, that same customer returns to place an order with your co-worker that outshines your proficiency for the entire year! No need to be perplexed as to what became of your treat. You gave it away by failing to remember that, "self-indulgence" is also Card 3's personal weakness. "Whenever the Empress comes to call, in your reading, you'd be wise to avoid any temptation to lull yourself into a false sense of security."

Now let's discover how the tests, rewards, and situations, indicated by Major Arcana Cards 11-22 the Fool, could impact your long-range goals, or destiny. For example: though relatively comfortable, your role in life has left you feeling dissatisfied and unfulfilled for some time. In todays reading you received Card 16 the Tower, and immediately begin to imagine what fresh calamity awaits you. Two weeks pass and nothing's changed. No calamity. No catastrophe. No bad news. Today, you receive a college brochure in the post. Yet, instead of chucking it in the dustbin, you read the information. Next week, you sign up for college and begin feeling more alive and inspired than you have in years. Within three years, you own your own company, as well as a lovely home and it appears you've just met the person of your dreams. From Card 16 the Tower:

Keywords: Karmic Upheaval. Personal Strength: reorganization. Personal Weakness: hesitation. "Now is an ideal time to begin reconstructing certain aspects of your attitude and behavior that have been preventing you from making the most of yourself" – and *that* was exactly what you did!

However, Major Arcana cards 2-10 also represent the higher vibration of Subject Cards 2-10[3], from the Minor Arcana[4]. The only difference is that while situations suggested by Cards 2-10 from the Minor Arcana are more spontaneous, matters concerning Cards 2-10 from the Major Arcana can help you make or adjust to changes that are more permanent. For example, with Tarot Dynamics, all 7's[5] correspond to the constructive, or self-defeating manner in which you handle or allow yourself to be handled by all your relationships.

Yet, when dealing with Card 7 the Chariot (from the Major Arcana) whatever occurs between you and other people will either make or have a stronger impression upon you, your relationship or your role in the relationship – perhaps even the manner in which you will view, and handle other relationships in the future. However, because Card 33 the Seven of Wands, Card 43 the Seven of Cups, 61, the Seven of Swords and Card 75 the Seven of Pentacles (from the Minor Arcana) often signify situations, advantages, opportunities, moods or obstacles in relationships that can come out of nowhere, they can also pass just as quickly, like a tempest in a tea-pot,

---

[3]With Tarot Dynamics the only Number 1 card is Card 1 the Magician.
[4]The Minor Arcana and Subject Cards are addressed in Chapter 2
[5]All 7's ; Card 7 the Chariot, The 7 of Wands, 7 of Cups, 7 of Swords & 7 of Pentacles

leaving matters or the relationship to carry on as before[6].

The more Major Arcana Cards there are in the spread the more emotionally or spiritually significant this reading will prove to be. The more often one particular Major Arcana Card appears in consecutive readings, the more you may need to call upon or work to develop the personal strength it represents. Depending upon your situation, it's not uncommon for as many as three Major Arcana Cards to reappear in several consecutive readings, and whether their definitions are encouraging you to pay more attention to a situation, or give more serious consideration to an opportunity, the longer you choose to deny, rather than apply your personal strength, the longer matters will either remain the same or in limbo.

KEY POINTS WHEN READING THE MAJOR ARCANA

Major Arcana cards represent Spiritual Karma, which we are forever resolving, creating and recreating, and "Karma" equals "cause and effect" – which can be as simple as knowing when to leave well enough alone, or finally stepping up to the plate to confront a matter that we've been avoiding.

---

[6]Imagine that nine cards in a ten-card spread (such as the Celtic Cross) are all quite positive and encouraging – except for one, which happens to be the Five of Swords. From Chapter 5 concerning the Five of Swords it says " The more encouraging the situation or other cards in the spread, the easier you can toss aside reluctance or self-doubt to address or proceed with matters you've been wondering or worrying about". So yes, the seeker is going to encounter a temporary wrinkle or dilemma. However, it is much less likely to present a major impediment. In most cases the entire incident will prove to be a "blessing in disguise" that enables the seeker to move forward more smoothly

Aside from their individual definitions each Major Arcana Card also corresponds to a simple personal strength, such as patience, or weakness, such as intolerance that will shortly be tested or rewarded –perhaps even strengthened or abolished by the upcoming situation.

Whatever tests, rewards or situation you encounter with Major Arcana Cards 1 through 10 tend to represent something you have earned through your recent behavior and actions, whereas situations indicated by Cards 11 Justice, through Card 22 the Fool, tend to have a greater impact upon your long-range, goals, endeavors and, sometimes even your destiny.

The more often one Major Arcana card reappears in your readings, the more you may need to call upon or develop the personal strength it represents.

The more Major Arcana cards there are in your reading, the more emotionally or spiritually significant your reading will prove to be, signaling a turning point in your perception.

THE MAJOR ARCANA
The Magician

The Magician can help you help yourself, to become a hero or a heel in the near future. Your willingness, or refusal, to apply your willpower constructively will reward, or undermine, your progress. The more definite your goals, the more resourceful your approach will be to any obstacle that threatens your progress. You won't be satisfied with giving less than your best now. Your need to prove yourself is very karmic. Each of your decisions and actions are designed to produce a definite effect. Emergencies as well as unexpected developments can create opportunities for you, if you're paying attention. You'll feel ready to handle anything, but be careful not to take on more than you know you can handle comfortably.

The more encouraging the situation, or other cards in the spread, the more likely you are to receive some type of recognition or reward for your efforts or services. A subconscious harmony between your intuition and the facts can make you more adept at "sensing" what's going to happen next in matters. Your determination to reach your goals can enable you to handle even the most delicate matters with a gentle detachment – getting to the point without making others feel offended or foolish.

The more challenging the situation, or other cards in the spread the more you may need to rely on yourself, and if so, learning to or letting yourself relax may be one of your biggest challenges. Trying to make yourself, and everything else so perfect, may be preventing you from enjoying your gains and loved ones as much as you deserve. The greater your success, or the closer you come to achieving it, the more you may fear it will disappear.

At your best, you're not afraid to stand alone. In fact, you may prefer to do so, or do your best work alone. By challenging yourself to make your best better, you can become as courageous as you are innovative. **However, should you be overstressed,** or the Magician appears in reverse, (upside down)

Card 1
The Magician

Keywords:
Karmic/Self-Reliance

Personal Strength:
Initiative

Personal weakness:
Impatience

For New Students:
Just like the 1st House in Astrology since our Magician is also synonymous with our survival instinct, he too, can sometimes strengthens our desire to succeed –at any cost.

you can become very impatient, even ill tempered in such a way that you thoroughly undermine matters for yourself through obsessive self-interest or total disregard for other people's opinions, advice or assistance.

With Card 1, your "self-reliance" is about to be tested or rewarded. So whatever changes, revelations or breakthroughs that occur are likely to prove more memorable – whether by causing you to feel more or less self-confident about trusting your own judgment, or perhaps as a reference point that you can (or will) look back upon and say "where I am now, stems from the day I decided to do (or say) that."

The High Priestess

Subconsciously, if not consciously, your emotions are lending a passionate, even sensual, impact that other people can feel and will respond to accordingly.

The High Priestess is capricious. When you're having a good day, you can easily attract positive attention and cooperation. On a bad day, without meaning to or realizing it, you could attract negative attention unless you are careful. During this time period your dreams may become more vivid or precognitive. Your personal and professional relationships (especially but not exclusively with women) will experience some degree of reconstruction and re-evaluation. Your likes and dislikes will be more noticeable. The better you feel about yourself and your life, the better you'll feel physically. The greater your irritation or dissatisfaction with yourself, or matters, the greater your vulnerability to illness, negative thinking and suspicion.

The more encouraging the situation, or other cards in the spread, the more reliable your intuition will be. Your desire to understand can make you more tolerant of others idiosyncrasies. Your knack for making the impossible possible could soon be your key to gaining some type of emotional, material, legal or even medical advantage.

The more challenging the situation, or other cards in the spread the more you need to monitor your moods and stick to the facts. If not, lending the impression that you're saying "maybe" instead of "no" could create unnecessary problems. Your desire to protect your loved ones, may be making your relationships more challenging than they have to be. Chance, rather than destiny, may bring a material inheritance or golden opportunity your way – but not without strings attached.

At your best, you will be uncommonly intuitive and compassionate. **However, should you be overstressed,** or the High Priestess appears in reverse, (upside down) you may be too

Card 2
The High Priestess

Keywords:
Karmic/Attachments

Personal Strength:
Insight

Personal Weakness:
Intolerance

For New Students:

Like the 2nd House in Astrology, despite her fondness for company, the High Priestess also triggers an awareness of how much we're recieving in return from other people and matters.

THE HIGH PRIESTESS

quick to change the rules in matters to suit yourself, whether to eliminate an obstacle, or to confound anyone that you perceive as competition. The inability to resist a little intrigue could bring more than you are prepared to handle.

With Card 2, your "insight" (or perception) is about to be tested or rewarded. Whether you'll soon need to re-evaluate a feeling, a belief, a promise or a goal, by listening to your inner-self now, you'll see matters more clearly and handle them more quickly, and effectively later.

The Empress

As long as you've been doing your best, you're certain to succeed with the matters that mean the most to you. Although the Empress can help smooth or improve your communications and develop new or better connections, she is not your "fairy godmother." So whenever she comes to call, in your reading, you'd be wise to avoid any temptation to lull yourself into a false sense of security. Being fond of the optimistic opportunist, she can and will enhance your luck, opportunity and talent as long as you're exerting honest and practical effort. The better you feel about you, the better your chances for attaining personal happiness, professional success or financial ease. The greater your self-doubts, the easier others can and may abuse your generosity or trap you in self-defeating situations. Self-indulgence may become your worst enemy, whether you're eating or exercising too much or too little, or becoming addicted to sex, gambling or substance abuse.

The more encouraging the situation, or other cards in the spread, the more likely you are to come closer to achieving you objective – if not actually attaining it. Your perseverance, and unshakable (though not always unwavering) faith in yourself and your goal, may soon light your way to success. Knowing that other people are counting on you can bolster your courage, resourcefulness and self-confidence.

The more challenging the situation or other cards in the spread the more diplomatic you'll need to be but the easier you'll devise effective strategies and achieve small advances that can make big differences in the future. Taking a short break can recharge your energy and renew your confidence in matters you were ready to abandon. Your sense of humor can enable you to "go with the flow" until you can turn the tide in your favor.

At your best, whatever the situation, your flexible nature enables you to remain focused upon your main objective,

Card 3
The Empress

Keyword:
Karmic/Thinking
and Networking

Personal Strength:
Optimism

Personal Weakness:
Self-Indulgence

For New Students:
Like the 3rd House in Astrology, the Empress also signals news, ideas and activity that can keep us in–touch and on our toes, or lead us to change our minds at the last minute.

LA EMPERATRIZ / DIE HERRSCHERIN **III** L'IMPERATRICE / L'IMPÉRATRICE

THE EMPRESS

when you're confronted by other challenges. **However, should you be overstressed,** or the Empress appears in reverse, (upside down) whereas self-indulgence could tarnish your reputation and achievements, apathy could trigger setbacks that put you on a much different path, than the happy one you envisioned.

With Card 3, your "optimism" is about to be tested or rewarded. The better you feel about you the more certain you are to succeed with matters that come to mean the most to you. Allowing egotism to masquerade as optimism can also pave the way to self-indulgence.

The Emperor

A control issue, at work, home or both, may bring your emotions closer to the surface or cause you to be more protective about your sense of belonging and security. The Emperor intensifies your need to discover the truth in all matters. Whatever the situation, your sense of belonging or desire for security will have a stronger-than-usual bearing upon your actions and behavior. The manner in which you choose to resolve your differences can exert a particularly karmic influence. The more challenging it is to complete matters to your satisfaction and everyone's best interest, the more important it is that you try to do so. Self-control and self-discipline are important to success. You may have to, or be asked to take charge of an important matter at work or at home. You're going to be a little more self-assertive and direct whether or not you'd planned to be.

The more encouraging the situation, or other cards in the spread, the greater your mental energy – but the more demands there may be upon your stamina. You can use your sense of humor to transform your less successful experiences into stepping-stones that instruct and inspire others. Your ability, to temper determination with diplomacy can help you get further ahead in matters, at a faster pace than even you expected. You may become somewhat of a legend or a role model due to your willingness to do, "whatever it takes," to set matters on course and keep them there.

The more challenging the situation, or other cards in the spread the harder it may be to gain control of things at home or work. Whether you're angry or worried, giving in to the temptation to make matters move faster than they should, or really need to, could make more, not less problems for you. An over abundance of intensity or self-righteousness may sentence you to social and emotional isolation. The greater your reluctance to accept a matter you cannot change, the easier inner turmoil could upset your physical well-being in ways, which may not be immediately obvious.

Card 4
The Emperor

Keywords:

Karmic/Belonging and Security

Personal Strength: Leadership

Personal weakness: Tyranny

For New Students:

Like the 4th House in Astrology the Emperor signals an increase or decrease in our material and domestic activities, which can strengthen or disturb our sense of belonging and security.

At your best, you will be ambitious, but not greedy, more concerned with delegating authority than flaunting it. **However, should you be overstressed,** or the Emperor appears in reverse, (upside down) you may become excessively, petty, controlling and demanding. Whatever the situation, you may discover that you've never really had as much control of matters as you believed.

With Card 4, your "leadership" is about to be tested or rewarded. *The Emperor* often appears at the beginning or end of a personally stressful or demanding episode when you need to exercise some additional self-control and common-sense.

The Hierophant

The Hierophant intensifies your creativity and sense of drama. The Hierophant tends to coincide with a time period that can prove to be uncommonly productive, or produce serious repercussions at a later time. If matters are going smoothly, you may be feeling bored and restless. However, if matters are not to your liking you could be too quick to blow things out of proportion or refuse to consider alternatives. You'll hate it if people don't take you seriously, but keeping whatever promises you've made can also make you feel as if you're being taken advantage of! Your desire to see the truth can become a double-edged sword, when the facts conflict with your desire to be the good guy. Meditation, yoga or attending your place of worship can help tame whatever inconsistencies or indecision, you may be wrestling with.

With The Hierophant you should always expect your professional, family and/or love life to become a little more adventurous and exciting as well as trying and demanding. You'd also be especially wise to choose your lovers and associates, more carefully now, as the Hierophant can also warn of an impending scandal, unkind accusation or rumors that may or may not directly involve you. Should this be the case, you may not be able to extricate yourself or your reputation from any unpleasantness, as quickly as you might become involved with it.

The more encouraging the situation, or other cards in the spread, the easier you can retain your focus and compromise or relate to other points of view, enabling you to "spice up" some of your relationships and simplify others.

The more challenging the situation, or other cards in the spread the more cheated and disheartened you'll feel by outcomes that fail to meet your expectations. Ongoing inconsistencies, in your behavior and communication could prove hazardous to your professional standing, as well as your emotional happiness. Should your moods dictate your spending habits, money problems may become a source of constant concern, whether you've created them or allowed others to create them for you.

At your best, you are freethinking, and free-spirited. Your sharp sense of humor and contagious nonchalance can and will

Card 5
The Hierophant

Keywords:
Karmic/Conflict and Speculation

Personal Strength:
Originality

Personal Weakness:
Procrastination

For New Students:
Like the 5th House in Astrology, the Hierophant can trigger an unexpected conflict of interest between our logic and emotions, in matters ranging from duty, to friendship, finance, romance - or parenting.

minimize tension, wherever you go. **However, should you be overstressed,** or the Hierophant appears in reverse, (upside down) you can become vulnerable to reckless, even dangerous behavior, without realizing it. Whatever the situation, you'd be wise to check and double-check your facts before taking matters any farther.

With Card 5 your "originality" is about to be tested or rewarded. The stronger your attraction to, or irritation with someone or something the easier you can convince yourself that the end will justify the means.

The Lovers

From broken dreams to broken hearts and everything in between, the Lovers is all about repairing whatever needs to be fixed or clarified! Your willingness, or refusal, to establish harmony between your ideals and life's realities hold the key to your happiness. Events developing now could enhance your awareness and understanding of others, in addition to your peace of mind. You need to feel proud of those you love and know that they're proud of you. You may meet one or more new people, who prove important to your future, or reconnect with someone from your past. However, the stronger your sense of responsibility, dedication or personal appeal – the easier you may also attract people that make it more, not less challenging to achieve your own goals.

The more encouraging the situation, or other cards in the spread, the more you and other people are likely to enjoy each other's company. The better you feel about yourself, the more mutually satisfying all your personal relationships will be; and your sense of humor, can prevent you from viewing any opinions that clash with yours, as a personal threat, or insult. You are sure to feel more playful, adventurous and spontaneous, as well as artistically – or academically creative. You may be nominated for an award or promotion, receive a bonus, special recognition, or an apology.

The more challenging the situation, or other cards in the spread, even your best relationships may encounter some strain or tension. Once you stop trying to be everything to everyone, or expecting others to be everything to you, the relationships that mean the most to you, will show a marked improvement. Continuing or beginning to repress rather than express your feelings could invite more, not less, trauma into your personal and professional life.

At tour best, your heightened awareness and understanding of others' will also help you achieve a better understanding of yourself. **However, should you be overstressed,** or the Lovers

Card 6
The Lovers

Keywords:
**Karmic/
Commitment**

Personal Strength:
Charisma

Personal Weakness:
Exploitation

For New Students:
Like the 6th House in
Astrology, the Lovers
can also signal
situations that could
disrupt or improve
our personal peace
of mind as we strive
to keep pace with
matters and people
that comprise our of
our daily routine, at
work and home.

appear in reverse, (upside down) you may become too sub-servient to others, too jealous or too certain that your charm alone will convince other people to see matters your way.

With Card 6, whatever the situation, your "charisma" is about to be tested or rewarded. You may meet one or more new people, who prove important to your future, or recon-nect with someone from your past.

The Chariot

Your attitude, moods and views, now have a stronger influence upon other people than you may realize. Certain events that develop will raise your awareness of the constructive or self-defeating manner in which you're moving through life. At this time, you're as much an emotional catalyst for the other people in your life as they are for you. To retain or establish better control of matters at work and home, you will have to play a dual role of follower and leader. You may even emerge as a follower who is becoming an effective leader or simply more independent. Issues relating to travel, as well as communication, could soon find you revising your personal, professional and financial strategies and schedules. If you're in the habit of driving too quickly or carelessly, there could be a traffic ticket in your near future, unless you're careful.

The more encouraging the situation, or other cards in the spread, the greater your efficiency and leadership will be. Any altercations you might encounter will bring you more opportunity than they will cost you. If relocation, or travel is on your agenda now, there's likely to be a romantic, adventurous or unusual story, behind it.

The more challenging the situation, or the other cards in the spread the more concentrated your advancement may need to be. At work and home your patience is sure to be tested, whether by annoying delays, miscommunication, mechanical breakdowns or a few medical inconveniencies. Confronting the worst in matters now, no matter how reluctantly, can help free the best in you.

At your best, whatever the situation, this is a time when you can intuitively choose the correct path in every instance, and keep matters moving along that path. **However, should you be overstressed,** or the Chariot appears in reverse, (upside down) the more strongly you believe that only one person or matter can make you happy or

Card 7
The Chariot

Keywords:
Karmic/
Relationships

Personal Strength:
Synergy

Personal Weakness:
Apathy

For New Students:
Like the 7th House in Astrology, the Chariot, can signal an unexpected turn of events, - for better or worse, concerning our relationships, at work, home or both.

EL CARRO
DER WAGEN
VII
IL CARRO
LE CHAR

THE CHARIOT

give your life meaning, the more likely you're looking for your self-confidence, in the wrong place. Whether due to circumstances beyond your control, or some type of personal miscalculation, at home, work or both, matters are less likely to proceed as smoothly or quickly as you had hoped.

With Card 7, your "synergy" is about to be tested or rewarded. One or more of your relationships are about to enter a new phase that that could open your eyes or broaden your horizons, if you're paying attention!

Strength

Strength is all about taking some timeout to recapture or reaffirm your peace of mind and confidence. Summoning your inner Strength will help you combat self-doubt when it threatens your peace of mind, and prevent you from creating additional problems through anger and/or frustration. Inner strength can help you meet virtually any challenge – even when you don't feel you can or you'd rather not try. Letting go of matters you can't change requires more strength than starting over. At this time there is a strong link between your physical and mental health. The stronger you are emotionally, the healthier you'll be physically and the better your chances of minimizing negative effects of minor illnesses. The stronger your motivation, the more vibrant your personality and the more resourceful your approach to tackling whatever obstacles may appear to be standing between you and your goals.

The more encouraging the situation, or other cards in the spread, the more easily your Faith will be rewarded with the peace of mind you deserve when you know you've done your best. Whatever your situation, now is the time when you can begin to transcend former weaknesses, bad habits, or self-doubts, more easily, much like a butterfly emerging from its chrysalis. Whether or not you've been aware of your intuitive abilities in the past, they may prove uncannily accurate now. You may return from a long walk, or a short drive, feeling completely rejuvenated because the answers that you set out to find, found you!

The more challenging the situation, or other cards in the spread the more fears of recrimination, rejection, failure, or being alone, can promote a tendency to settle for what comes the easiest in matters – even when it's not what you want or deserve.

At your best, you are more open to exploring new places, methods and ideas in a manner that is as organized as

Card 8
Strength

Keywords:
Karmic/
Renovation

Personal Strength:
Fortitude

Personal Weakness:
Fear

For New Students:
Like the 8th House in Astrology, Strength can also provide clues concerning the stability of our future, with anyone or anything that is important to us.

it is realistic. **However, should you be overstressed,** or Card 8 Strength appears in reverse, (upside down) you may be too quick to blame other people, or see and hear only what you want to. Refusing to let go of matters that went wrong in the past could cheat you out of a productive and happy future.

With Card 8, your "fortitude" is about to be tested or rewarded, and whatever the situation – on some level your best can still become better.

The Hermit

Karma is working through circumstance to help you tie up any loose ends you've been avoiding. Although the Hermit will sometimes test your beliefs, and understanding in ways and at times that surprise you, it also offers you additional spiritual protection and enhance your awareness, in times of stress or crisis. Taking the time (perhaps through meditation) to integrate your spirituality and intuition could save you from the lesser elements in yourself as well as last-minute physical danger. People's actions will speak much louder than their words. The more you listen, the more you'll learn. This is a good time to pursue self-enlightenment whether through travel, or perhaps even private or group study, as a student or even a teacher. The more you rely on your common sense and the less you rely on others to keep their word, the more often you'll make the choices and decisions, that are best for you and what you hope to achieve.

The more encouraging the situation, or other cards in the spread, the easier you can expand your philosophical and intellectual outlook, and plan your advancement in matters. At this time, your ability to sense what other people are about to say, do, need or want may be almost spooky. Your ability to see others, yourself, and matters now, for what they really are, can help you reach or re-align your goals more quickly and easily. **The more challenging the situation,** or the other cards in the spread the easier and more effectively you can communicate with people – while keeping your distance and biding time, like a general planning a campaign. Your mind is as versatile as it is durable. However, the more attention you devote to one matter, the easier you could lose touch with, or track of, another.

At your best, you can reduce the most complex data, to something everyone can understand. You're always pondering ways and means to gain additional insight. **However, should you be under pressure, or Card Nine appears**

Card 9

The Hermit

Keywords:

Karmic/ Understanding

Personal Strength: Logic

Personal Weakness: Irrationality

For New Students:
Like the 9th House in Astrology, the Hermit can also make it easier or more of a challenge to expand our outlook, while maintaining our beliefs and self-confidence.

in reverse, (upside down) you could go out of your way to provoke controversy, or a showdown (that you can't win) with other people. If so, you may also discover that you don't know quite as much, as you believed.

With Card 9, your "logic" is about to be tested or rewarded. The Hermit can both keep your goals and conscience in synch, by helping you make sound choices and decisions based upon logic, rather than emotion, thereby enabling you to view your past experiences, present situation and future goals from three distinct vantage points, the philosopher, the politician and the prophet.

Fortune's Wheel

Taking a fresh perspective may be your ticket to success by making your best even better. Fortune's Wheel is a kaleidoscope. When you view matters from one angle, you can see numerous advantages and opportunities through the challenges. Yet, the slightest shift in the angle introduces a completely different picture. Your attitude and behavior will generate a great deal of "instant" karma that can immediately change the course of issues hanging in the balance. Material dilemmas can help strengthen you emotionally, and emotional dilemmas can help you become more resourceful materially. Sometimes, making the wrong choice may even prove to be the right move that launches you towards victory. The greater your willingness to do more than your fair share in matters, the greater your chances of success. The longer you focus on matters that are going against you, the longer it takes to see the opportunities Fortune's Wheel is trying to show you. **The more encouraging the situation,** or other cards in the spread, the easier you can take charge and make changes that will make things even better than you expected. The more realistic your goals, the easier you can prevent frustration from running away with your peace of mind. The sooner you utilize your personal strengths, the easier and more quickly you can win against any problems, whether you've created them or allowed others to create them for you. When it comes to helping people you care for, you can move mountains now!

The more challenging the situation, or other cards in the spread the more important it is not to punish new opportunities for past mistakes you've made. Fortune's Wheel can enhance your luck in small ways that you may take for granted or consider too insignificant. A situation or event that doesn't immediately go your way could prove to be a blessing in disguise.

At your best, you're a self-starter, as confident in your ability to handle your own concerns, as you are ready and willing to help others when, and where you can. **However, should**

Card 10
Fortune's Wheel

Keywords:
Karmic/
Achievement

Personal Strength:
Confidence

Personal Weakness:
Imprudence

For New Students:
Like the 10th House in Astrology, since Fortunes Wheel can also lead us to feel as if we're closer too, or farther away from achieving our goals it can also make whatever we're doing more or less enjoyable.

you be overstressed, or Card Ten, Fortune's Wheel appears in reverse, (upside down) impatience and intolerance for even the kindest suggestions or most constructive criticisms, could keep you on the inside track to nowhere.

With Card 10 your "confidence" is about to be tested or rewarded. Although Card 10, Fortune's Wheel will *occasionally* accompany a "lucky win or big break" it has a greater propensity for appearing anytime you're in danger of expecting too much or too little from life as well as yourself.

Justice

Justice can enable you to take new matters in stride, without unbalancing the other issues in your life. You'll need to make certain adjustments, whether to accommodate the unexpected, please yourself and others you care for, or to accommodate a loss. Life is a little less inclined to overlook mistakes you make now. You also may be less tolerant or patient. In some instances Justice can indicate an approaching (or ongoing) legal concern.

As a rule, however, Justice represents your need to restore or establish better balance in your daily routine, whether you've been taking on too much – or not enough lately. Consciously, subconsciously, or both, you're simply more concerned about what's fair for you. In times of trial, Justice can sometimes nudge your conscience and help you make the right decision, even when you'd prefer not to – or it can become more difficult to apologize or admit your mistakes. Depending upon the situation, Justice can occasionally render you more vulnerable to manipulation, from the people you trust, – especially family and friends.

The more encouraging the situation, or other cards in the spread, the easier you can reorganize your agenda to meet your obligations and insure your peace of mind. The sooner you stop taking yourself for granted, the sooner others will too. The better you feel about you, the less reluctant you'll be to bring any unpleasant episodes to an end. Whatever the situation, the more comfortable you are with yourself, and your goals, the less you'll worry about making the first move, and the less time you'll waste worrying about nonsensical things that could go wrong.

The more challenging the situation, or the other cards in the spread the more effort it may require to extricate yourself gracefully from certain issues.

At your best, no matter how great the temptation, your sense of honesty and fair play will prevent you from committing

Card 11
Justice

Keywords:
Karmic/Balance

Personal Strength:
Integrity

Personal Weakness:
Impudence

For New Students:
Justice reminds us that what goes around, does indeed come around. The more comfortable you are with the truth, the less judgmental you will be concerning yourselves, others, or both.

actions you might later regret. **However, should you be under pressure,** or Justice appears in reverse, (upside down) you may be too quick to make mountains out of molehills, or take offense where none was intended. Whatever the situation, a prejudicial attitude, coming from you or towards you, will only serve to confuse matters.

With Card 11, your sense of integrity is about to be tested or possibly even rewarded. The greater your self-doubts the more likely you are to follow bad advice, or leap before you look. The more comfortable you are with yourself, the sooner and easier you can distinguish the important from the trivial in matters and people to make and uphold the decisions that are best for you.

The Hanged Man

The more objectively you view yourself and matters, the more you stand to gain. Retaining an objective attitude now can also boost your physical and emotional defense systems. Consciously, subconsciously, or both, you've been taking a different view of many things, people and yourself that is leading to a spiritual transformation. Even now, your new perspective is helping you make more sense of current matters, so that you can make peace with the past, and re-evaluate your goals for the future, with greater clarity. You may choose to further your self-enlightenment through group or private study that could include meditation or yoga.

The more encouraging the situation, or other cards in the spread, the easier it will be to make realistic decisions and achieve your goals. Tranquility can prevent your spirit from being broken by any setbacks or delays you may encounter. Best of all people, will be unable to make you feel guilty when you know you don't deserve to.

The more challenging the situation, or the other cards in the spread the more likely you are to make self-sacrifices that accomplish nothing and prove nothing of value. The greater your self-doubts the more likely you are to follow the path of least resistance whether or not, it's best for you or the situation. The easier you can hide your frustration with one matter, the harder it will be to avoid taking out your resentment on other matters and people who don't deserve it. Each loose end you choose to overlook in one matter will eventually resurface in another.

At your best, you can view your best and worst experiences, as friends who enable you to continually bring out the best in yourself and matters. **However, should you be under pressure,** or the Hanged Man appears in

Card 12
The Hanged Man

Keywords:
**Karmic/
Tranquility**

Personal Strength:
Composure

Personal Weakness:
Passivity

For New Students:
Being a steadfast
believer in the
promise of
tomorrow, the
Hanged Man
can lend you
whatever patience,
perseverance (or
both) that you need
to remain focused
on today's goals.

reverse, (upside down) no matter how ready you are to begin taking steps in a better direction you could still fall back too quickly and easily into self-limiting habits and attitudes.

With Card 12, your sense of composure and objectivity are about to be tested. As long as you understand that you can't have matters both ways, The Hanged Man will enable you to make realistic decisions and retain the focus you need to prioritize and achieve your goals.

Death

The better the opportunity, or the greater the challenge, the stronger your will to survive, the easier you can re-invent yourself, like the Phoenix rising from the ashes. Should it seem that the stronger your desire to succeed, the harder it is to decide what you want to do, and where you should begin, by unleashing your ability to separate your feelings from the facts you'll discover that you can make even the most difficult choices and decisions more easily now. This technique can also help ease your mind and clear your conscience of pointless guilt over matters you might have handled differently, even though you know it would not have changed anything for the better.

The more encouraging the situation, or other cards in the spread, the more security oriented you are, ready and able to provide your own inspiration and motivation. You're not afraid of compromise and, if necessary, you'll work hard to achieve one that's comfortable for all parties. You can end an emotional relationship, without sacrificing the friendship, or easily resume a friendship from long ago. You're flexible enough to accommodate any unpredictable twists in matters that might arise.

The more challenging the situation, or other cards in the spread, the greater your temptation to dwell upon unpleasant matters and create excuses that keep you at war with yourself, your opportunities and other people.

At your best, you're always open to new ideas and useful information that can help you reach the top in any endeavor. **However, should you be under pressure, or Death appears in reverse,** (upside down) you could become be too self-contained, preferring to walk out instead of talk out your differences. Whatever your reasons, the longer you choose to remain in denial, or resistant

Card 13
Death

Keywords:

**Karmic/
Transformation**

Personal Strength:
Regeneration

Personal Weakness:
Stagnation

For New Students:
Whatever the circumstances, you can't function well or happily now, in atmospheres that are too stagnant, confining or uncertain. Despite it's name, Death is a more frequent companion of opportunity than tragedy.

to making changes that could eventually improve your situation, the longer matters will remain in limbo.

With Card 13, your powers of personal self-regeneration are about to be tested. Whether materially, emotionally, physically or psychologically Card 13 can enable you to reach the top, in any endeavor – or find a better path, as soon as you are ready.

Temperance

Whatever your situation, compromise and moderation will prove to be your Guardian Angel. No matter what our goals, it's the routines we adopt to achieve them, which can literally transform our lives.

The more encouraging the situation, or other cards in the spread, and the more determined you are to win, the more often your fantasies can supply the energy you need to cope when things seem impossible. Your sense of humor can help you realize how much your smaller "trials and tribulations have helped strengthen your character. In some instances, making or taking the time, to initiate a frank and open discussion where everyone can "agree to disagree" without endangering their relationship will prevent people from feeling that you are pushing or judging them. If nothing else, clearing the air will ease your mind.

The more challenging the situation, or other cards in the spread the stronger your temptation to remain chained to people and matters that are wrong for you by telling yourself it's for your own good or the sake of others. Bad relationships can become a bad, but convenient habit, even an excuse for not making the most of yourself, and taking your own talents for granted. Physically, the harder it is for you relax, the more susceptible you may be to mysterious rashes and other annoying more than life-threatening illnesses.

At your best, you're a realist at heart, always ready, eager and willing to expand your horizons, one step at a time. **However, should you be overstressed,** or Temperance appears in reverse, (upside down) your dreams may prove more precognitive, but difficult to interpret. Whatever your situation, you are likely to be more easily distracted

Card 14
Temperance

Keywords:

Karmic/ Compromise

Personal Strength:
Forbearance

Personal Weakness:
Misjudgment

For New Students:

Like you, Temperance can be as challenging as it is invigorating to deal with! Mastering the art of self-compromise will enable you to realize that even your smallest victories are stepping stones towards greater clarity and achievements.

than usual. Impulse, rather than intuition, could even lead you to say, do or possibly even, purchase something you could regret.

With Card 14, on some level, your "forbearance" is about to be tested. You may be pleasantly surprised, to discover that you have been the only person who was demanding too much from yourself.

The Devil

The stronger your determination to get your way in matters, the easier you can talk yourself (or anyone else) into whatever suits your purpose. Whatever your situation, summoning the self-control that you need to defeat petty temptation now, may prove more challenging than you expect. Your instincts for emotional and material gain are very strong, and you must choose whether to let them lead you in the right or wrong direction. If you've been minding your P's and Q's, you're sure to encounter a spot or two of good luck or "flashes" of creative ingenuity that could save you in the nick of time. However, if you've been pushing your luck too far, rather than work through situations, there'll be hell to pay!

The more encouraging the other cards in the spread, the easier you can summon the self-control and self-discipline you need to defeat petty temptations, and perhaps even accomplish the impossible. Common sense can keep your enthusiasm and optimism in check to prevent you from taking on more than you can handle. The more strongly you desire personal recognition, or achievement the more accurately you can perceive other peoples' merits' and intentions.

The more challenging the situation, or the other cards in the spread the greater your susceptibility to procrastination, taking foolish chances, or behaving in a manner that will do you more harm than good. Your desire to be desired, or to be of service to others is balanced against a fear of being used, or that other people will simply expect too much.

At your best, your devilish sense of humor, and easygoing manner will allow you to appear calmer and more confident than you feel when you're under pressure. Your conscience is a tough taskmaster that prevents you

Card 15
The Devil

Keywords:

Karmic/Obstacles

Personal Strength:
Decency

Personal Weakness:
Vulnerability

For New Students:

The majority of any obstacles confronting you now are more likely to be self-induced, such as commitments you've undertaken, boasts or promises you've made (perhaps in haste) that you must now live up to.

from lying to yourself. **However, should you be over-stressed,** or the Devil appears in reverse, (upside down) The temptation to push yourself beyond your limits can lead you to mistake a no-win situation for just another challenge.

With Card 15, on some level, your sense of "decency" is about to be tested. Whether you're being tempted, or tempting others the more excuses you make, the more obstacles you'll create.

The Tower

Now is an ideal time to begin rebuilding any aspects of your life or behavior that may have been preventing you from making the most of you and your life. In some manner, your ability to let go of things you still want – but no longer need, will be challenged. Physically, you could be your own worst enemy now by neglecting your physician's advice, or waiting too long to seek medical attention. Emotionally, you may need to be a little more flexible to accommodate growing pains in you or your relationships. Professionally and materially, the more you're forced to accomplish on your own now, the more successful you're likely to become.

The more encouraging the situation, or other cards in the spread, the easier you can tackle self-doubts. You are likely to issue some statements that surprise others. The more you can appreciate knowing the facts in matters now, the more quickly and easily you can make whatever changes are necessary to insure your mutual, or personal security and continuity.

The more challenging the situation, or the other cards in the spread the more likely you are to hear something you won't like, or the harder you may try to hang onto matters that are not as good for you as you're trying to believe they are. A tendency to tell other people only what you feel they need to know could lead to an avoidable misunderstanding.

At your best, the less you can do about one matter, the more strongly you'll focus on making advancements in others'. **However, should you be overstressed,** or the Tower appears in reverse, (upside down) viewing yourself as a "victim of circumstances" will allow you to temporarily ignore the fact that you put yourself in that

Card 16
The Tower

Keywords:

Karmic/Upheaval

Personal Strength:
Reorganization

Personal Weakness:
Hesitation

For New Students:
To successfully tie
up any loose ends
in matters now, you
must believe that your
positive efforts are
never wasted–even
when you don't achieve
the desired results as
quickly as you'd hoped.

position. Then again, the longer you continue to focus
on only what you wish to see, the less satisfied you'll be
with everything and everyone else. Refusing to accept
things you cannot change can make you your own worst
enemy.

With Card 16, in one or more ways, way your "reorga-
nizational skills", are about to be tested and the Tower
can help clarify your perception of matters, as well as
yourself!

The Star

The stronger your Faith in a higher power, the easier hope can refresh and rejuvenate your life now. You are infused with a conscious or subconscious need to know that can help you achieve your goals. Even if it feels as though hope is all you have, it will also be everything you need to motivate yourself. There are billions of stars in the sky. Some glow weakly, some flare brilliantly for a short time and some shine steadily. So it is with you now as you grow in ability, knowledge and understanding.

You sense that something is approaching, and you're on the verge of a personal transformation. This is a good time to seek or further clarification through meditation, yoga, or attending your place of worship more regularly. Without even trying, you can now draw additional strength and energy from the moods and attitudes of the people who comprise your daily routine. The stronger your feelings for them, the stronger your intuitive link to them will become. You may even know when a loved one or friend needs you, before they contact you.

The more encouraging the situation, or other cards in the spread, the easier it will be to get in touch with your inner-self and allow your intuition to guide you. Your dreams may also reinforce your spiritual and emotional co-ordination. An unsettling circumstance that forces you to confront reality could also be the gateway to your greatest personal, or mutual achievement.

The more challenging the situation, or the other cards in the spread the more surely you will be tested on your ability to believe that there is a positive purpose behind even the most trying matters. You may seek further clarification through professional counseling.

At your best, your best luck will stem from your willingness to heed sound advice and follow your own higher instincts. At work and home, your calm and rational approach can help everyone retain their focus upon the matters at hand.

Card 17

The Star

Keywords:

Karmic/Hope

Personal Strength:

Faith

Personal Weakness:

Self-Deception

For New Students:

With Card 17, the greater your expectations, the harder it can be to accept delays and disappointments, but the sooner you can recognize the difference between a healthy challenge, and a no-win situation, the smoother your path will be.

However, should you be overstressed, or the Star appears in reverse, (upside down) since you're presently as emotional as you are intuitive, an overabundance of any emotion could cause you to misinterpret your intuition.

With Card 17, your "Faith", whether in yourself, other people or something that you have come to believe, is about to be tested. The more open you are to new possibilities, the more likely your faith will be rewarded – though perhaps in a manner and time when you least expect it.

The Moon

One or more matters in your life will soon need to be examined more closely. Your emotions are restless. Your intuition is keen. Whatever the situation, being honest with yourself and others now, really is the best policy. If you are feeling melancholy, irritable, suspicious or anxious and unable to pinpoint the exact source of your distress, you may soon hear several pieces of bad news from or about people you know and care for. If you cannot and have not been able to shake your melancholy now is a good time to consult with a professional counselor or religious advisor. The more constructively you channel your emotions now, the better all your endeavors will fare. Physically, you may more susceptible to nervous upsets and ailments that can be a by-product of stress. Emotionally, the more you feel you need to be needed to feel good about you, the more vulnerable you are to slights and criticisms.

The more encouraging the situation, or other cards in the spread, the easier you can relax by doing things you enjoy. This will allow solutions to your problems to come to you and prevent you from taking out your frustrations on others or yourself.

The more challenging the situation, or the other cards in the spread the more likely you are entrenching yourself in denial, about your job, health or relationships. This self-defeating cycle aligns your energy, fears and anger against each opportunity you have to change things for the better.

At your best, by working with whatever new facts "come to light" now, you can be particularly innovative concerning matters from finance to romance, and everything in between. **However, should you be overstressed, or the Moon appears in reverse,** (upside down) any matters you may have been hiding (or hiding from) as well as

Card 18
The Moon

Keywords:
Karmic/Caution

Personal Strength:
Vigilance

Personal Weakness:
Avoidance

For New Students:
Card 18, marks the beginning of a new or different emotional cycle in connection with your domestic and material concerns that can make it more or less challenging to know what you really want or to remain focused on matters at hand.

some that have been hidden from you, are more likely to be revealed. Whatever the situation, you can too easily become overwhelmed by emotional or material preoccupations, that could prove counterproductive to what you hope to achieve.

With Card 18, since your "vigilance", is about to be tested, so the delicate balance between your emotional perspective, material assets and opportunities is subject to change without notice.

The Sun

Whatever the situation, you are likely to feel quite optimistic, or simply find it easier to view matters in a more positive light. Your ambitions are like Pandora's box. The effort you expend to achieve them will unleash greater challenges and opportunities than you expect. Success can be yours, no matter what the challenge by expending the right balance of energy, ambition, and emotion. Taking the time to combine your willpower with patience will enhance your creativity and resourcefulness enabling you to easily move mountains. The manner in which you respond will begin to reveal each person or situations purpose in your life and your purpose related to them, like the rising sun.

The more encouraging the situation, or other cards in the spread, the easier you can attract and influence other people. This is a time for sharing and receiving good news, from job to romance, pregnancy and everything in between. In tense moments, adopting a non-judgmental manner can help everyone relax, and enable you to get great results from even the most difficult people. You can count on a resourceful network, of friends and acquaintances to provide you with good connections and information.

The more challenging the situation, or other cards in the spread the more you can count on some type of bright spot to see you through matters even if you are (or have been) courting physical, emotional or professional burn-out. Don't allow your stronger brighter self to be eclipsed by self-doubt or trying to impress or save the people and situations that are wrong for you.

At your best, the more comfortable you are with yourself now, the less likely you are to encounter any serious friction in your relationships at work, home or both. **However, should you be overstressed,** or the Sun appears in reverse, (upside down) a narcissistic temperament, coupled with a bad temper can emerge. Whether you're expecting too much too soon, or simply trying too hard in matters now,

Card 19
The Sun

Keywords:
Karmic/
Enlightenment

Personal Strength:
Congeniality

Personal Weakness:
Frustration

For New Students:
Card 19 can enable
you to realign your
goals and perspective
more easily and
realistically.
However, the greater
your impatience to
proceed with matters,
the more challenging
it may be to uphold
your new resolutions
or handle your
personal power as
wisely as you should.

the possibility of experiencing some type of personal burn-
out in the near future is higher than usual.

With Card 19 your "congeniality" is about to be tested, yet even
frustration with what you consider to be the worst in matters
can become the catalyst, that brings out the best in you.

Judgment

Judgment leads us to question the wisdom of continuing or beginning a certain course of action or behavior. Certain issues that you thought you'd resolved, as well as some you've been avoiding, will be resurfacing. Whether these issues concern your perspective, your feelings, your health, your goals, your job or your relationships, something will force you to make decisions or face facts you'd rather avoid. Just remember that no matter how inconvenient their arrival, new facts, developments or information you receive can also prove to be blessings in disguise, whether by offering you a chance to be your best, better, or by preventing you from making an even bigger mistake.

The more encouraging the situation, or other cards in the spread, the easier it will be for you to resolve matters and clear the air without incurring additional misconceptions. You may soon receive some type of vindication or exoneration possibly even the means to transform what appears to be a disaster into an absolute success.

The more challenging the situation, or other cards in the spread the longer it may take to resolve matters. However, until you do resolve matters your endeavors will remain in limbo or out-of-step. You may feel that tying up loose ends is the story of your life. Whether you seem to keep starting over from the bottom of the ladder, or a little closer to the top, depends upon whether you're really learning what you need to know. Procrastination, rather than bad luck may be your biggest enemy.

At your best, the more in tune you are with yourself the easier you can rely on your own logic and rationality to arrive at the best decisions, despite outside pressure from others' opinions and suggestions. **However, should you**

Card 20
Judgment

Keywords:
Karmic/
Revelation

Personal Strength:
Patience

Personal Weakness:
Antagonism

For New Students:
With Card 20, the more you think you know what you're going to do and where you're going to go, the more likely you'll soon change your mind and direction.

be overstressed, or Judgment appears in reverse, (upside down) putting some distance between your emotions and the facts could improve your judgment and prevent you from making the wrong choice or move. If not, you may be too quick to notice and blame other people's mistakes without ever recognizing your own.

With Card 20, in one or more ways, your "patience" is about to be tested. The more you absorb and work truths you cannot escape, the more improvement you will see.

The World

The World is all about fresh starts and second chances. The less willing you are to free yourself from bad habits or emotional dependencies, the less good they will do you. The World celebrates forgiveness. How to forgive others, how to accept forgiveness and (most importantly) how to forgive yourself so that you can make the fresh start that leads to a happy ending. Since your freedom to act and react as you see fit, are especially important to you now, this is ideal for starting anything new from an attitude, to a diet and exercise program, to job or relationship and everything in between.

The more encouraging the other cards in the spread, the easier it will be for you to uphold your new resolutions and enjoy life. The better you feel about yourself and whatever you're doing, the easier you can coerce your opponents and achieve your own ends more peacefully. You can coax opportunity, to come to you now, simply by being yourself. Medically and even legally, you just might move mountains now.

The more challenging the situation, or other cards in the spread the more challenging it will be to use the pressure you're under to launch yourself in a better direction instead of falling back into the same old rut. Everything that you fail to start for the right reasons will never become what you envision, no matter how hard you try.

At your best, whatever your situation, because your needs and interests are expanding at a faster pace, you can be more of a self-starter than usual, or ever before. One or more fortunate business, social or romantic connections or opportunities may even come your way, like magic! **However, should you be overstressed,** or the World appears in reverse, (upside down) you'd be wise to beware the temptation to overextend your budget, or

Card 21
The World

Keywords:
Karmic/ Freedom

Personal Strength:
Enthusiasm

Personal Weakness:
Impracticality

For New Students:
With Card 21, in many larger and smaller instances at work and home, you could emerge as a leader now– setting the pace and blazing new trails, which could improve one or more of your relationships at work, home or both and boost your self-confidence.

overstep your emotional boundaries. Whatever the situation, you could become too daring, or devious in ways that can make other people uneasy.

With Card 21, in one or more ways, your "enthusiasm" is about to be tested. So giving yourself something positive to look forward to, and setting goals that more realistic than idealistic will make you feel more alive than anything else can.

The Fool

Whether or not you'd expected to, you're about to embark upon a new chapter in life. The more headway you see you are making matters now, the more you stand to gain by practicing cautious expansion. Consciously, subconsciously, or both, you're ready and willing to take more responsibility for your own success and happiness. Whether you're about to begin or seek a new job, make a change in residence (or changes within your residence), begin or end a course of study – or a relationship, you're going to experience new (or renewed) self-confidence. You're relying on you more than ever to make your dreams come true. You may be traveling more or meeting new people in the near future.

The more encouraging the situation, or other cards in the spread, the easier you can put your new plans in motion. This is a marvelous time to cultivate introductions and establish, or renew acquaintanceships with people whose professional or even political standing might open some doors for you. Professionally and financially, the greater your determination to succeed, the sooner your focus will shift from merely gratifying your immediate desires, to perfecting your talents and creating your own opportunities. If you're in the market for romance, treating yourself to a vacation or changing your social habits in the near future, could be the catalyst that sets your social or love life back on track.

The more challenging the situation, or the other cards in the spread the more likely you may be fooling yourself again, or simply trying to impress or save the wrong people.

At your best, you will immerse yourself in every aspect of whatever you are doing. At work and home, you will be uncommonly resourceful and patient in your quest to achieve the best results. **However, should you be overstressed,** or the Fool appears in reverse, (upside down) whatever your situation, beware impatience and over optimism. Your quest for personal gain or achievement may cause you

Card 22
The Fool

Keywords:
Karmic/
Motivation

Personal Strength:
Common Sense

Personal Weakness:
Overconfidence

For New Students:
With Card 22, as long as you remember that nothing in life is "fool-proof" you won't lose your balance between fantasy and reality – especially (but not only) when tackling any loose ends in matters.

to lose touch with reality, as well as the needs and feelings of other people. Too late, you may realize that you're living in a fool's paradise.

With Card 22, in one or more ways, your "commonsense" is about to be tested, and by listening to your intuition, working with your talents, respecting your convictions and replenishing your determination, you CAN make the impossible possible.

ABOUT THE MINOR ARCANA

Function: To tell The Story Behind The Major Arcanas Headlines

Keywords: Change, Emotion, Challenge, Ambition

Minor Arcana cards reveal matters that are or will be happening now.

CHAPTER 2

The Minor Arcana (whose name translates into "Small Secrets") reveals the most likely type of situation that will reward and test the personal strengths of the Major Arcana Cards. For instance, should Card 43 the Three of Cups appear in today's reading and you already plan to attend a party Saturday night you may not feel impressed if your reader mentions it. Yet, the fact that it was mentioned, means that attending that party will prove more significant than you are aware. Why? Because you're going to have more or less fun than you expected, whether or not the reader provides specific details. Elsewhere in the reading,(depending upon the cards that accompany Card 43) you may hear you'll soon meet someone new or be "under the weather". You could meet that "someone new" after the party or through another party guest. You might contract a cold or the flu from someone else that attended the party. Readings are like life – it's the smaller episodes that make the biggest differences!

The Minor Arcana contains four elemental suits of cards, the Wands[1], Cups[2], Swords[3] and Pentacles[4], which will be addressed individually in chapters 3 through 6. Every suit consists of 14 cards, and each suit relates to one of the four elements that comprise our natural world, as well as the Astrological building blocks, Fire, Water, Air and Earth.

So while the following information will prove to be particularly helpful for anyone with a desire to work more closely with the Tarot, it is an invaluable asset in bringing to life any of the many exquisite 78 Card

---

[1] Wands equal Change
[2] Cups equal Emotion
[3] Swords equal Challenge
[4] Pentacles equal Ambition

Tarot decks whose Minor Arcana Subject Cards feature symbols[5], instead of pictures.

ABOUT COURT CARDS

Court Cards ALWAYS trigger some form of personal regeneration, or degeneration. (i.e. backsliding)

In Tarot Dynamics, the first five cards in each suit of the Minor Arcana are the King, Queen, Knight, Page and Ace. Collectively, they are known as the Court Cards. As a student, I was taught that (for instance) the Ace[6] of Wands represented the Kingdom (or State) of Change and Chaos, in which all Wands reside", while the Knight[7] of Wands, served as the trailblazer and defender of the realm. Naturally, the King of any suit made the laws, while their Queen kept "order in the court" and each Page (sometimes called knave, Prince or Princess) was nothing more than the town crier, tattletale or gossip. Since the King or Queen, of any suit never represented any more than grand opportunity or someone blocking your path, it's not surprising that the basic definition and description for each Court Card revolved around the possibility of hearing about or making contact with a person of interest, or merit.

However, not everyone is going to have a family emergency, reunion, make a new best friend, begin a new romance, lose or find a job, or suddenly become embroiled in some type of legal difficulty, simply because a King, Queen, Knight or Ace appears in their spread. Nor is

---

[5] such as, four Cups floating in the air.

[6] Aces were a means to identify a situation that was on the Seeker's horizon or in their recent past. Wands = change and/or instability. Cups = a very emotional time or situation. Swords = a very busy and/or challenging time or situation. Pentacles = a time emotional and economic gain or loss.

[7] Whatever their suit, the Knight symbolized aggression coming from or towards the Seeker.

everyone who receives a Page about to hear of a wedding, pregnancy or begin planning a small trip. Although Court cards *sometimes* imply closer involvement or contact with influential people such as close friends, older people or authority figures, they *always* trigger some form of personal regeneration or degeneration (i.e. back-sliding!) – for better or worse, at work, home or both. More pleasant examples would be, planning a wedding, preparing to interview for a new job or better position, even making plans to relocate.

Less pleasant but also applicable examples: planning legal strategies, or trying to mend a relationship. Little things *do* mean a *lot*. Blending the more personal or human function of each Court Card, with its' basic keywords and definitions enables the more experienced reader to round out the scope and accuracy of their reading. It also provides an essential starting point that students can relate to more easily and, saves new readers, who are still learning to trust their intuition, a great deal of frustration. Better yet it enables us to clearly see the bigger picture that means the most, to you or whomever you are reading for.

ABOUT KINGS

All Kings trigger or enhance your initiative.

Yes. Kings can sometimes indicate an impending disagreement or reconciliation at home or work, or that a new man is on your romantic horizon, concern for the health or happiness of a male relative, or that someone will soon contact you concerning a new job or better position. More often than not, however the appearance of a King in your spread indicates, that you will soon need (or want) to play a more important role or assume more responsibility in your daily routine, whether to keep, or get matters moving. The elemental suit (Wands, Cups,

Swords or Pentacles) that governs each King also lends you specific behavioral advantages that can quickly and easily provide the upper hand you need to achieve a goal, or mount a solid defense. So, in addition to the keyword that governs their elemental suit each King shares the keyword, Initiative.

The King of Wands, = Change(able) Initiative.

The King of Cups, =Emotion(al) Initiative

The King of Swords, = Challenging Initiative

The King of Pentacles, = Ambitious Initiative

Whatever your gender or situation, in keeping with their suit, all Kings trigger or enhance your personal initiative and leadership, whether to set new wheels in motion or handle an ongoing situation more effectively. For example: you wish to approach your spouse or partner about a matter concerning your relationship, but due to your busy work schedules, you can't find the right time or moment. Today, Card 37 the King of Cups appears in your reading. Tomorrow, you arrive home from work bearing flowers, a small gift and announce that you've made reservations for the weekend at a new bed-and-breakfast! The more encouraging the situation – as in our example the more strategic your maneuvers and methods will be. The more challenging the situation (if for instance you're in the midst of a divorce) the less self-control you may exert, acting and reacting without regard for the consequences.

The more Kings you see in your spread, whether or not men or authority figures will soon play a more significant role in your progress, your behavior and moods are about to undergo some rapid changes. For instance: your nature is generally very thoughtful and easy-going. However, in yesterdays reading, you received the King of Swords, the King of Wands and the King of Pentacles. The next morning you feel and behave as if you are simply waiting for someone to make a mistake (King of Swords). That afternoon you simply can't make up your mind about anything (King of Wands), but come the evening, you're in a great mood (King of Pentacles) and can't understand why everyone around you appears to be "walking on eggshells"!

ABOUT QUEENS

All Queens can enhance your people and coping skills.

Yes. Queens can sometimes indicate an impending disagreement or reconciliation at home or work, or that a new woman is on your romantic horizon, concern for the health or happiness of a female friend or relative, or that someone will soon contact you concerning a new job or better position. More often than not however, the appearance of a Queen in your spread indicates that you will soon need (or want) to play a more diversified role, whether in managing or cultivating situations. For instance, three weeks ago you were elected to spearhead a community campaign that's scheduled to begin three weeks from now. Shortly after your election, what appeared to be a small disruption in your family began to escalate and required additional attention from you. Now all is well.

When Card 52 the Queen of Swords appeared in yesterdays reading, you could not understand why. This morning, you suddenly realize there are only three weeks until the campaign begins. Having made no appointments or arrangements thus far, you must immediately spring into action now, and so begin the process of negotiating and bargaining your way to the top (with the florist, the caterer and other volunteers), which is one of the best qualities, the Queen of Swords has to offer! The elemental suit (Wands, Cups, Swords or Pentacles) that governs each Queen strengthens your ability to gradually make the most or best of matters, by lending you a charismatic appeal that can charm, coerce or even reveal your detractors. Since "Charm" corresponds to each Queens best line of defense or offense, in addition to the keyword that governs their elemental suit each Queen also shares the keyword, Charm.

The Queen of Wands = Change(able) Charm.

The Queen of Cups =Emotion(al) Charm.

The Queen of Swords = Challenging Charm.

The Queen of Pentacles = Ambitious Charm.

Whatever your gender or situation, in keeping with their suits, all Queens, trigger or enhance your personal charisma, people, and coping skills, so that you may manage matters more effectively. The more encouraging the situation the more likely you can provide a positive source of inspiration upon everything and everyone around you. The more challenging the situation the more likely you could instigate chaos to get your own way. The more Queens you see in your spread, whether or not women will shortly play a more significant role in your progress, or peace of mind, your people and coping skills will need to be especially flexible, in the near future.

ABOUT KNIGHTS

Knights indicate unexpected developments in matters and your behavior.

In keeping with their suit, every Knight has the potential to stimulate a different type of personal behavior that can lead you to say or do something you hadn't planned on, simply because Knights are reactionaries. They inspire us to either reformulate our strategy or take a matter to the next level. However, since any change you make in one matter will require that you make a change in still another, Knights also tend to trigger a "domino" effect.

For example, it's February and you plan to purchase a new automobile in October. In today's reading you receive Card 67 the Knight of Pentacles. Next week, the car that you fancy becomes available for a great deal less than you'd planned to pay, although the cost is still more than you can presently afford. Upon examining your current expenditures, you realize that by canceling your vacation, reducing your food budget, trimming your entertainment allowance and not purchasing a new cell phone, you can afford to purchase the car now.

Yes. A Knight can sometimes indicate a young man or woman over the age of sixteen, but under the age of twenty-five, or a close call with danger or disappointment, perhaps even a heroic rescue or a new admirer that will sweep you off your feet. More often than not however, the appearance of a Knight in your spread indicates the approach of unexpected developments. Whatever your gender or situation, the best or worst of each Knights energy is a set in motion by your perception of people and matters that stand between you and what you hope to accomplish. While each Knight shares the keyword "Adventure", they also govern the season of their suit. Memorizing these seasonal factors can aid your intuition and improve your accuracy in timing the beginning or ending of more eventful situations and time periods.

Knight of Wands = Spring &Change(able) Adventure.

The Knight of Cups = Summer & Emotion(al) Adventure.

The Knight of Swords = Fall & Challenging Adventure.

The Knight of Pentacles = Winter & Ambitious Adventure.

The more encouraging the situation the more the more quickly and effectively you can continue dealing with new developments as they arise. The more challenging the situation the longer and harder you may have to work to stay on top of matters or to defend your position. The more Knights you find in your spread the more likely your plans will be interrupted by a combination of pleasant as well as annoying interludes.

ABOUT PAGES[8]

Pages signal small matters with the potential to grow larger – a work in progress.

Yes. A Page can sometimes represent, children, grandchildren or pregnancy, special invitations, welcome or unwelcome news and company, as well as taking or planning a short trip. More often than not however, Page's represent the figurative "birth" of new idea, option, or a set of circumstances that you hadn't considered before.

So in addition to the keyword that governs their suit each Page shares the keyword, Surprise, which refers to the type of experience you are most likely to encounter or initiate.

The suit that governs each Page, can lend you a fresh perspective and outlook that enables you to make even the most challenging decisions and choices more easily.

The Page of Wands = Change(able) Surprises.

The Page of Cups =Emotion(al) Surprises.

The Page of Swords = Challenging Surprises

The Page of Pentacles = Ambitious Surprises

Whatever your gender or situation, each Page, signals small matters with the potential to grow larger – a work in progress, in keeping with their suit. For example:

---

[8]a.k.a. Prince, Princess or Knave in some Tarot Decks

last year, you undertook a new hobby, building ships-in-a-bottle. Now, you're considering the possibility of turning your hobby into a part-time job, but don't know where to begin. In yesterdays reading the Page of Pentacles appeared. There's no possibility of you having another child and your grandchildren are much too young to consider marriage. Your full-time job is secure, and you have neither the desire nor hope for further advancement in your present career. Next Sunday, while welcoming new neighbors, you discover that they own a hobby shop, and would be delighted to feature your craftwork on consignment, and suggest that you might even conduct a class or two!

Your hobby has been a "work in progress" and while the offer you received is a small matter now – it has the potential to grow larger. The more encouraging the situation the easier you can make the most of small surprises, opportunities and ideas that can make big differences for the better in your future. The more challenging the situation, the easier you might make mountains out of molehills. The more Pages you find in your spread, the more different types of news, information and gossip you can expect to receive – so be sure to check your sources before you pass along any secrets or rumors that you hear.

ABOUT ACES

Aces signify an inevitable showdown.

Aces are the Tarot's way of measuring your personal growth, and each Ace embodies the purest form of the element it represents. Whatever your gender or situation, they indicate that an inevitable showdown, is approaching, whether with yourself, matters or other people. For example: you hope to be an author, but fearing rejection you've been procrastinating about submitting your proposal to a publisher. Yesterday, the Ace of

Wands appeared in your spread. This morning you suddenly decide that, "come what may" you must mail your submission. Three months later, the Ace of Swords and Pentacles appear in your spread. Next week, you receive a letter of acceptance along with a request, to contact the publisher a.s.a.p. to discuss your contract!

In addition to the keyword that governs their elemental suit each Ace also shares the Keywords Crisis or Reward, which refers to the type of experience you are most likely to encounter or initiate.

The Ace of Wands = Change (through) Crisis or Reward

The Ace of Cups = Emotional Crisis or Reward

The Ace of Swords = Challenging Crisis or Reward

The Ace of Pentacles = Ambitious Crisis or Reward

So whether you're about make a break, experience a breakthrough, or seek professional advice or assistance to resolve a medical issue or curb a bad habit, Aces signify a major, sometimes even an unique turning point in your life. The better prepared you are to begin a new undertaking the easier (if not sooner) you begin making the most of your new opportunity or circumstances. Yet, even more upsetting situations will be accompanied by a "eureka" moment of crystal clarity when you realize that you are better off, or better equipped to handle matters than you expected. The more Aces you find in your spread, the more likely you are approaching a major turning point and the more you stand to gain or lose through your own behavior.

KEY POINTS WHEN READING COURT CARDS

All Kings trigger or enhance your initiative leadership, whether to set new wheels in motion or handle an ongoing situation more effectively.

The more Kings there are in your spread, the more likely your behavior and moods are about to undergo some rapid changes.

All Queens enhance or trigger your people and coping skills.

The more Queens you see in your spread, the more you will need to rely on your people and coping skills in the near future.

All Knights indicate unexpected developments in matters and your behavior.

While Knights inspire you to either reformulate your strategy or take a matter to the next level, they also trigger a domino effect. So whatever change you make or encounter in one matter often requires making or confronting a change in yet another matter.

The more Knights there are in your spread the more likely your plans will be interrupted by a combination of pleasant as well as annoying interludes.

All Pages signal small matters with the potential to grow larger – a work in progress, from pregnancy to the birth of a new idea or options that you had not considered before.

The more Pages there are in your spread, the more different types of news, information and gossip, or visitors you can expect to receive.

Aces signify an inevitable showdown, whether with you, matters or other people.

Aces are the Tarot's way of measuring your personal growth.

With every Ace, even upsets will be accompanied by a "eureka" moment of crystal clarity when you realize that you are "better off", or better equipped to handle matters, than you expected.

The more Aces there are your spread, the more you stand to gain or lose through your own behavior.

ABOUT SUBJECT CARDS

Whether or not they bring good tidings, Subject cards have a stronger impact upon your immediate agenda, which is what holds the key to your future.

No one was more surprised than I to discover that the label, "Subject Cards" has become "lost-in-the-shuffle" of the Minor Arcana. I was taught to regard the Tarot Cards labeled 2 through 10 of every suit as being the servants (or subjects) of the Court Cards, and just like any Royal Court the King, Queen and Page of every suit each had their own personal retainer. For instance, just as the King of Wands relied upon the Two of Wands for reinforcement, the Queen of Wands depended upon the Three of Wands to enhance her charm and sharpen her people skills, while the Four of Wands alternated between keeping the Page of Wands focused and amused. Naturally, this same (two, three, four) pattern[9] of servitude repeats itself through all four suits cards. Although I have not found these combinations to accompany circumstances that are more fortunate or unfortunate I have found that they can produce a more resourceful or detrimental effect upon our moods which always impacts our approach and handling of matters - for better or worse.

WANDS:

In terms of personal initiative because Card 28 the Two of Wands is second only to Card 23 the King of Wands whenever they appear together, they can be one of the

---

[9]King of Cups and Two of Cups, Queen of Cups and Three of Cups, Page of Cups and Four of Cups, King of Swords and Two of Swords, Queen of Swords and Three of Swords, King of Pentacles and Two of Pentacles, Queen of Pentacles and Three of Pentacles, Page of Pentacles and Four of Pentacles.

most self-constructive or self-destructive combinations in the Tarot.

When it comes to choosing the right time, opportunity and people, the Three of Wands is second only to the Queen of Wands. So, anytime they appear together, they can be one of the most vivacious or vicious combinations in the Tarot.

As far as organization and timing the Four of Wands is second only to the Page of Wands, which can make them one of the most straightforward and well-organized or haphazard card combinations in the Tarot.

CUPS:

In terms of emotional initiative, since Card 42 the Two of Cups is second only to Card 37 the King of Cups, anytime they appear together, they can be one of the most credible and compelling or conniving and controlling combinations in the Tarot[10].

When it comes to fact-finding, the Three of Cups is second only to the Queen of Cups – and since neither of them is ever without an agenda when acquiring or delivering information, they can be one of the most sensitive and intelligent or deliberately inconsiderate and tactless combinations in the Tarot.

Concerning sound material and emotional organization, the Four of Cups is second only to the Page of Cups. So, anytime they get together, they can be one of the most focused and perceptive or naïve and inconsistent combinations in the Tarot.

SWORDS:

In terms of mental and psychological agility and initiative, the Two of Swords is second only to the King of Swords,

---

[10]For more information concerning these combinations see the "Lunar-Tarot Guide" in Chapter 10.

so together, they can be one of the most efficient and inspirational or confusing and distracted combinations in the Tarot.

As far as mental and psychological understanding, the Three of Swords is second only to the Queen of Swords and anytime they appear together, they can be one of the most universally enlightened or personally embattled combinations in the Tarot.

In terms of mental versatility and agility, the Four of Swords is second only to the Page of Swords, which makes them one of the most organized and patient, or unfortunately impulsive combinations in the Tarot.

PENTACLES:

In terms of practical accord and initiative, the Two of Pentacles is second only to the King of Pentacles, so anytime they appear together, they can be one of the most shrewd, dependable and self-disciplined or self-involved, undependable and irresponsible combinations in the Tarot.

When it comes to practical achievement, the Three of Pentacles is second only to the Queen of Pentacles, which makes them one of the most ambitious, persistent and creative, or selfish, meddle-some, and stubborn combinations in the Tarot.

In terms of practical accord and initiative, since the Four of Pentacles is second only to the Page of Pentacles when-ever they get together, they can be one of the most thoughtful and well prepared or depressive and indecisive combinations in the Tarot.

However, this also left Subject cards five through ten simply waiting in the wings. For example: since it was customary to read and regard the King or Queen of any suit as either a glorious possibility or someone blocking your path, so should Card 31 the Five of Wands appear with the King or Queen (of any suit) the Five of Wands was always signal to fight fire-with-fire, whether to claim a prize or withstand a challenge. Why? Simply because whatever the situation, Wands *always* urged or warned of aggression. Swords were always synonymous with employing, or resisting cunning and stealth. Cups were nothing more than love and family, being won or lost, while Pentacles could only imply financial, professional or material goods being won, stolen or squandered.

Simply reading the Court Cards as significant "future possibilities", while reading the Subject cards, as the most effective ways and means to handle those "possibilities" (should they arise), seldom prepares you for what actually lies ahead. How are you to know "when, how, what, where and why" you might expect the "possible" treat or calamity, that might be triggered by the Court Cards? Throughout history, from government to parent-hood, it's always the "subjects" that keep bosses on edge, and on their toes. So it shouldn't be such a surprise to discover, that the Subject Cards can, and often do, call the tunes to which the Court Cards dance, whether with delight or frustration – and usually a bit of both!

Most 78 Tarot Card decks contain 22 Major Arcana Cards, and 56 Minor Arcana Cards. Yet, since the Minor Arcana, contains 20 Court Cards, (which do operate on a more personal level) there are only 36 true subject cards.

Unless a Subject card is traveling with Court Cards or Major Arcana Cards they often signify situations, moods, opportunities or obstacles that will tend to come and go more quickly – like a tempest in a tea-pot. For example, tomorrow morning, rather than read your horoscope, you decide to draw one Tarot Card. Much to your chagrin, you've selected Card 57 the Three of Swords. Oh, woe. Your good mood begins to sour as you begin to worry and wonder "what if", concerning your job, your family and your friends. Time to go to work, and your car won't start – your battery is dead. You've known that you needed a new one, but hoped it could wait till next weekend. Fortunately, the bus stop is on the corner of your street. While you wait, a co-worker drives by, offers you a ride and so you arrive on time for work after all. At lunchtime, the vending machines refuse to accept the bills from your wallet, and you have no coins.

Suddenly, another coworker invites you to share a pizza. It's almost time to go home, when you realize you're missing an important file and may have to work late, call a cab to get home and cancel an important social engagement. Suddenly, the missing document is discovered and your evening is back on track again! Yes. The Three of Swords does signal some degree of delay, disappointment, loss, or even a series of smaller upsets, which you experienced. However, just as in our example those events often stem from nothing more than personal miscalculation – a tendency to over and underestimate matters, people or both. So you see, although sometimes we must act more quickly upon whatever opportunities, or emergencies accompany Subject Cards 2-10, it's also best to avoid taking unexpected upsets too seriously – without thinking them over. Yes. Subject cards 2-10 do have a stronger impact upon your immediate agenda, but it's how you choose to handle your immediate agenda, that can open or close certain doors to your future.

Working with the subject at hand, to produce a successful conclusion is what life is all about. Getting the best out of a subject, without letting it get the better of you is an art! Successfully changing a subject is always more difficult than giving way to self-pity or submitting to it's unreasonable demands.

KEY POINTS WHEN READING SUBJECT CARDS

Subject Cards 2 through 10 (from any suit) tend to signify situations, advantages, opportunities, moods or obstacles in relationships that can come out of nowhere, and often pass just as quickly, like a tempest in a tea-pot. So although you must sometimes, act more quickly upon whatever opportunities, or emergencies they bring, it's also best to avoid taking unexpected upsets to seriously – without thinking them over.

This simple formula will enable you to begin reading your Subject cards more quickly and easily.

Their number (2-10) will reveal **where** you can expect to encounter a new development.

Their suit will reveal **what** type of development you can expect.

Their definition reveals your options and most beneficial approach to surmounting or coping with matters.

Now let's explain **HOW** Subject cards 2-10 can reveal where you can expect to encounter a new development. For Instance:

Each 2, will correlate to your attachment to someone, something – or both.

All 3's correspond to your mindset and thinking.

Every 4 relates to your security and sense of belonging.

All 5's correlate to your ability to spice up, or simplify some matters, as well as your desire to suit yourself or do the right thing.

Every 6 corresponds to meeting and improving some aspect of your daily commitments and routine.

Each 7 (whether directly, or indirectly) will always pertain your relationships.

All 8's relate to your future.

Every 9 corresponds to your understanding.

Each 10 is all about what you have achieved and/or hope to achieve.

Now let's see WHY the suits can reveal what type of development you can expect:

Wands signify a change of plans. **Cups** represent an emotional development. **Swords** indicate a more challenging development. **Pentacles** suggest an ambitious development.

Now let's see how your definitions can enable you to discover your best options or approach to surmounting or coping with matters.

For example, all 6's correspond to your level of commitment to your wellbeing and daily routine. So, should you see Card 60 the Six of Swords, you can expect something to impact your daily routine, for better or worse. Although "Challenge" is the keyword for the entire suit of Swords, they can also bring order into chaos. So just as the Number 6 helped you identify **where** to expect a new development, the suit reveals what type of development you can expect, and **how** you might handle it more easily. Concerning your options, *which depends upon your situation*, in Chapter 5, the Six of Swords says, "whether you need to stop making excuses or stop accepting them, now is the time to find a better way to handle yourself and matters." Then too, "if travel is on your agenda, you may revisit someplace from your past, or someone you enjoy may unexpectedly reappear in your life."

About Subject Card 2

TWO REPRESENTS INTERACTION and ATTACHMENTS

"Attachments" refers to the fact that your level of attachment to someone or something, such as a habit, routine, project or object, is about to increase or decrease.

Just like the 2nd House in Astrology and Card 2 the High Priestess, the Second subject card (of any suit) also deals with achieving and maintaining better balance and control of your emotional and material goals. Yet despite its fondness for company, 2's also contain an element of self-interest and self-preservation that can increase or decrease your level of attachment to matters and people – according to how much you feel you are receiving in return –from family, friends, your employer, your material investments – even a course of study or medical treatment. Their suit will reveal whether you'll find it easier or more challenging to interact constructively with other people. Should the number "2" repeat itself in your reading, you may need to consult more people than you expected, or more people, than usual, may request favors or advice from you. The more encouraging the other cards, the easier you can gain whatever assistance, approval or co-operation you may require. The more challenging the other cards the more resistance or delays you are likely to encounter.

About Subject Card 3

THREE REPRESENTS THINKING and NETWORKING.

"Thinking and networking" means that YOUR mindset and moods will have a stronger-than-usual bearing upon how you will absorb and react to whatever is happening around you."

Just like the 3rd House in Astrology and Card 3 the Empress, third Subject card also correlates to how you absorb and react to what-ever is happening around you at home and at work – from get-togethers to emergencies. 3,s bring news and activity that can stimulate or curtail activity. In addition to describing what type of communication you are most likely to commence or encounter, their suits also indicate whether your mindset, or manner of self-expression is likely to prove more harmful or beneficial to your communications. The more 3's there are in your reading, the more your success will depend upon your ability or refusal to "think before you react" in matters. The more encouraging the other cards, the more rewarding or revealing your communications will be, and the easier you can meet your obligations or tackle emergencies that might arise. The more challenging the other cards, the more resistance or delays you may encounter in traveling as well as delivering and interpreting ideas and messages.

Subject Card 4
FOUR REPRESENTS BELONGING and SECURITY.

"Belonging and Security" refers to the fact that YOUR sense of personal belonging and security will have a stronger-than-usual influence upon how you choose to handle matters now."

Just like the 4th House in Astrology and Card 4 the Emperor, the fourth Subject card also corresponds to your sense of personal security and belonging, which impacts your incentive for beginning, completing or quitting matters. 4's often indicate an increase in our material and domestic activities that can strengthen or disturb our sense of security. Their suits will reveal whether you're ready to launch new projects, or hoping to hide from matters you don't wish to confront. Should the number 4 repeat itself in your spread, your peace of mind may soon be called into question. The more encouraging the other cards, the easier you can complete matters to your satisfaction and everyone's best interest. The more challenging the other cards, the longer you may procrastinate or the more resistance you may encounter.

About Subject Card 5
FIVE REPRESENTS CONFLICTS and SPECULATION.

Since 5's correlate to your desire to suit yourself, and still do the right thing in matters "Conflict and Speculation" explains why accepting or initiating any type of change may not come easily to you."

Just like the 5th House in Astrology and Card 5 the Hierophant, the fifth Subject card also represents your desire to be noticed, loved, and appreciated. 5's are "wild-cards" that can to trigger a conflict of interest whether between your logic and your emotions, you and someone else or, between what you should do and what you want to do. Their suits will indicate whether your efforts to get your way will prove more rewarding or exasperating. The more 5,s that you see in your reading, the more adversity or temptation you are about to encounter, so the more you may need to rely on your originality, creativity and flexibility. The more encouraging the cards, the easier you can bring forth the best in you and your endeavors by calling upon your self-control and self-discipline. The more challenging other cards, the harder you may make matters on yourself due to self-doubt or indecision.

About Subject Card 6
SIX REPRESENTS COMMITMENT.

"Commitment refers to your willingness to make whatever repairs may be necessary to keep matters running more smoothly and efficiently – sometimes by simply refreshing your perspective."

Just like the 6th House in Astrology and Card 6 the Lovers, the sixth Subject card can also signal situations that can enhance or disrupt our personal peace of mind as we strive to keep pace with matters and people that comprise our daily routine. From our attitude to our health and everything in between 6's have a knack for providing opportunities to fix or repair matters. That's why it's also important to remember that whatever we choose to do, say, or avoid today, will become tomorrows stepping stones or stumbling blocks. Their suits can assist you in determining whether it will be more or less enjoyable, easier or more challenging to meet your or break your current commitments as well as any new endeavors you may be considering. Any time more than one 6 appears in your spread, the busier your schedule will be. The more encouraging the other cards, the easier you can attain and maintain a constructive focus and routine. The more challenging the other cards the more likely you are to encounter a little more resistance or some additional delays in what you hope to accomplish.

About Subject Card 7
SEVEN REPRESENTS YOUR RELATIONSHIPS.

"Relationships" explains where you can expect your synergy, reliability, and flexibility to be tested or rewarded."

Just like the 7th House in Astrology and Card 7 the Chariot, the seventh Subject card also correlates to whether you're erecting and maintaining relationships that are mutually constructive, and interdependent, rather than co-dependant. 7's can signal an unexpected turn of events in our personal and professional goals and agreements. Their suit will enable you to determine whether now is your time to shine or revise your strategy. Should there be more than one 7 in your reading, you'd also be wise to take less for granted now in your relationships at work and home. The more encouraging the other cards the easier and farther your peopleskills can take you. The more challenging the other cards in the spread, the more resistance or delays you are likely to encounter in your relationships.

About Subject Card 8
EIGHT IS A CARD FOR FUTURE RENOVATION.

"Renovation" refers to opportunities and situations that have, or could potentially change your life."

Just like the 8th House in Astrology and Card 8 Strength, the eighth Subject card also deals with opportunities and situations that have or could change your life. It can offer clues about your future with anything or anyone that is valuable to you, such as, the stability of your relationships, your source of income, as well as your health and the health or prosperity of those you care for. Their suits will indicate whether you'll find it easier or more challenging to preserve or improve matters. Anytime more than one 8 appears in your spread, the more work you may have ahead of you – but the more encouraging the cards the easier or more enjoyable your tasks will be. The more challenging other cards the more resistance or delays you are likely to encounter until you're ready to readjust your focus or priorities and possibly both.

About Subject Card 9
NINE REPRESENTS YOUR UNDERSTANDING

"Understanding", refers to your willingness to expand your horizons. When you change the way you look at things, the things you look at change."

Just like the 9th House in Astrology and Card 9 the Hermit, the ninth subject card also test's or reward your beliefs, values and understanding – in ways, and at times that surprise you and crystallize your individuality. They can assist you in tying up whatever loose-ends could be impeding your progress as well as any you've been avoiding. So, whenever the Number 9 repeats itself in your reading, you may soon need to re-examine certain aspects of yourself, matters or other people. Their suits will reveal whether you'll find it easier or more challenging to expand your outlook for the betterment of matters. The more encouraging the other cards, the more quickly and easily you can reach a better understanding of yourself and other people. The more challenging the other cards in the spread, the more complications and contradictions you may have to unravel to achieve your better understanding.

About Subject Card 10
TEN REPRESENTS ACHIEVEMENT

"Achievement" corresponds to your desire for success, recognition, or both!

Just like the 10th House in Astrology and Card 10 Fortunes Wheel, the tenth and last subject card also corresponds to your desire and opportunities for achievement. 10's can also make us more aware of who we are, and how far we've come that can make whatever we're doing more or less enjoyable and whatever we hope to accomplish appear more possible or impossible to achieve. However, any time you discover more than one 10 in your reading, it can also generate a great deal of "instant karma" that can suddenly change the course of matters, for better or worse, through your behavior and attitude. Each of their suits indicates the manner in which you could create or cost yourself the outcome you desire. The more encouraging the other cards, the easier you can adjust your attitude and behavior to insure the outcome you desire. The more challenging the other cards, whether or not you like the outcomes that you devise, will be secondary to your willingness to deal with them constructively.

KEY POINTS WHEN READING SUBJECT CARDS

Subject Cards tend to signify situations, advantages, opportunities, moods or obstacles in matters and relationships that can come out of nowhere, and often pass just as quickly. Although you must sometimes, act more quickly upon whatever opportunities, or emergencies they bring, it's also best to avoid taking unexpected upsets too seriously – without thinking them over.

When Reading Subject Cards:

Their number (2-10) reveals *where* you can expect to encounter a new development.

Their suit reveals *what* type of development you can expect.

Wands = Changing Developments

Cups = An Emotional Development

Swords = A Challenging Development

Pentacles = A Practical Development

Their definition reveals your best options and approach to surmounting or coping with matters.

ABOUT WANDS[1]

Keyword: Change

Element: Fire

Corresponding Astrological Signs: Aries ♈, Leo ♌ and Sagittarius ♐.

Corresponding Playing Card: Diamonds.

Function: Wands can help you accept the necessity of making some changes and adapt to others.

---

[1] aka. Rods, Staffs, Staves, Acorns, Batons, Candlesticks etc., in other Tarot Decks

CHAPTER 3

In Tarot, the element of Fire corresponds to the suit of Wands as well as the Astrological Fire Signs, Aries ♈, Leo ♌ and Sagittarius ♐. Just as Fire blazes new trails, Wands and Fire Signs signify a desire to blaze your own trail, and often enhance your determination to win, one way or another. Taking a chance when you see that the time is right can enable you to blaze a new or better trail, that can turn the tide of matters in your favor. However, under more stressful conditions, like Fire, Wands can also trigger impulsive behavior that undermines your cause or leaves you feeling burned out. Wands imply change that can lead to personal renewal. Wands represent spontaneity, sudden gains and opportunity – or opposition that may come out of nowhere. The more encouraging the situation, the easier and more quickly you can make certain changes and prevent others from unbalancing your agenda. The more challenging the situation the less likely you are to make all the changes you'd hoped to and the more you need to beware of depleting your energy and encountering personal burnout. Should Wands comprise the majority of your spread it will prove more challenging to predict a definite outcome, as you are about to enter a very active, adventurous or possibly annoying time period. Your need to accommodate incoming changes, at home, work or both may limit the number of changes you can make. Resist the temptation to let your temper get the better of you; the more willing you are to work with matters, the more you will benefit later from everything you do and learn now.

KEY POINTS WHEN READING WANDS

All Wands correlate to the Astrological Fire Signs, Aries, ♈, Leo ♌ and Sagittarius ♐.

Wands can help you accept the necessity of making some changes and adapt to others.

"Changeable" suggests an upcoming necessity to make some changes and adapt to others.

Wands signify a desire to blaze your own trail, and often enhance your determination to win, one way or another.

Wands imply change that can lead to personal renewal.

Wands represent spontaneity, sudden gains and opportunity or opposition that may come out of nowhere.

However, under more stressful conditions, Wands can also trigger impulsive behavior that undermines your cause or leaves you feeling burned out.

Subject Cards 2-10 often signify situations, advantages, opportunities, moods or obstacles that come out of nowhere, and sometimes pass just as quickly.

THE WANDS
The King of Wands

Good or bad, the King of Wands makes his own luck, and so can you! Although you can be more impatient than you appear, you can also be particularly resourceful when you're under pressure. Material ease or professional acclaim, as well as emotional happiness can be yours, though they may not manifest in the time or manner you expect.

The more encouraging the situation, or other cards in the spread, the more energetically and enthusiastically you will approach each task and/or dilemma you encounter. At work and home, your ability to take charge of matters, and complete them in less time than you expected, may even surprise you! Your sense of humor is the perfect compliment and companion for your self-assertion, enabling you to impress and convince other people effortlessly. Meetings or interviews with authority figures are likely to go better than you'd hoped.

The more challenging the situation, or other cards in the spread the harder it may be for you to control matters or your temper. Meetings or interviews with authority figures are likely to prove counterproductive. You will begin more matters (and possibly more disagreements) than you can or really care to complete. You may make impulsive changes that you could regret later.

Romantically: Should your spread contain a hint of romance, you may suddenly develop an attraction for someone you've just met or known for awhile and go out of your way to gain their attention – perhaps without realizing it. **The more reassuring the situation,** or other cards in the spread, the ease with which you can accept and respect the differences in each others personalities could be the key ingredient to a lasting relationship. **The less reassuring the situation,** or other cards in the spread the more likely your attraction (or relationship) will burn itself (and you) out.

At your best, you earn other people's respect and affection in a manner that is as positive as it is productive. Your time

Card 23
the King of Wands

Kings trigger or
enhance your initiative.

Keywords:

Changeable/
Initiative

For New Students:

Whatever your gender
or situation, the King
can enable you to set
new wheels in motion,
or handle ongoing
situations more
effectively–whether to
gain an upper hand in
matters or mount a solid
defense.

REY DE BASTOS   RE DI BASTONI
KÖNIG DER STÄBE   ROI DE BÂTONS

KING OF WANDS

is well structured, whether you're putting together a new project or dashing to attend a class. **However, should you be overstressed or the King of Wands appears in reverse** (upside down) your initiative may be misdirected. The easier other people try to make matters for you, the harder you make matters for yourself. In an instant your moods can become too intense, dramatic, or extreme, causing you to embarrass yourself and others.

The King of Wands enhances your intuition, intensity and passion about everything and everyone you care about, which can inspire you to either become more fearless and pioneering, or simply rash and impulsive.

The Queen of Wands

Your people skills will be one of your greatest keys to success. Professionally and materially the fact that you can be an excellent judge of other people's potential and character is generally accompanied by a knack for steering matters and opinions in your favor. However, your attraction to and for people who inspire your imagination and curiosity can sometimes invite more intrigue than adventure into your personal realm. **The more encouraging the situation,** or other cards in the spread, the easier you can enlist other people's cooperation and charm their sensibilities by your positive example. At work and at home, you will encounter less opposition concerning even the most radical changes you make. This is an excellent time to gain an introduction to people who can further your interests. You may even negotiate a successful truce between opposing factions at work, at home, or both.

The more challenging the situation, or other cards in the spread the less charming you will feel and appear. The harder you try to mask your anxiety or irritability, the more obvious and contagious it becomes. You could start trouble between other people without being aware of it.

Romantically: Should your spread contain a hint of romance, whether or not you're aware of it, your desire to be noticed and appreciated will increase – enhancing your romantic powers of attraction. **The more reassuring the situation,** or other cards in the spread, the more likely you are to attract a wide variety of suitors, whose goals and personalities compliment your need for change, sense of adventure or both.

The less reassuring the situation, or other cards in the spread the more likely you are to make a nuisance of yourself, alienating not only the object of your affection but possibly a friend or two as well.

At your best, your enthusiasm is as charismatic as your confidence, and your keen powers of visualization can enable

Card 24
the Queen of Wands

**Queens can enhance
your people and
coping skills.**

Keywords:

Changeable/Charm

For New Students:

Whatever your gender,
or situation the Queen
can enable you to
keep everyone and
everything "on the
same page" more easily
by managing people
and cultivating matters
with greater efficiency.

you to work wonders. **However, should you be over-stressed,** or the Queen of Wands appears in reverse, (upside down) the close link between your emotions and your pride can interfere with your objectivity and wreak havoc in all areas of your life, or your charisma may simply attract the wrong elements.

Card 24 can enable you to steer matters and opinions in your favor, or simply arouse your penchant for speculation and extremism. Whatever your gender, or situation, your people and coping skills are about to be tested or required -perhaps in ways and at times that could catch you off guard!

The Knight of Wands

Whatever the situation, you need to be more observant of what's happening around you now, and do you best to stay flexible. All Knights are reactionaries. Each Knight has the potential to stimulate a different type of personal behavior, and the Knight of Wands can enable you to meet and make unexpected changes, more resourcefully.

The more encouraging the situation, or other cards in the spread, the easier you can turn any potential disadvantage into an advantage. At work or home, you will be less reluctant to adopt the attitude you need to accomplish things properly. Your flexibility and spontaneity may even surprise you, enabling you to discover more options and choices than you expected.

The more challenging the situation, or other cards in the spread the more your patience will be tried by petty annoyances, interruptions and other people's lack of consideration at work and at home. You may waste more time or money than you'd intended or more than you can afford on a matter. Events may force you to speak up for yourself – which could help clear the air or earn you respect – but only if you watch what you say and how you say it. Try to be more careful when traveling too; allow yourself extra time to reach your destination.

Romantically: Should your spread contain a hint of romance, the more likely you are to suddenly begin or end a romantic pursuit or relationship. **The more reassuring the situation,** or other cards in the spread, the more likely you are to accept a date with someone whether or not you'd been hoping they'd ask. You may even surprise yourself by making the first move! You could suddenly decide to become a couple with a current – or previous date-mate. **The less reassuring the situation,** or other cards in the spread the more tempting it may be to take a romantic risk that you will regret sooner than you think.

At your best, you can "go with the flow" when prudent, or swim confidently against the current when necessary, to reach your goals now. "Can-Do" is your motto! **However, should**

Card 25
the Knight of Wands

Knights indicate unexpected developments in matters or your behavior.

Keywords:

Changeable/ Adventure

For New Students:

Since Knights tend to trigger a "domino" effect, whether it's more expedient to move forward or step back for now, any changes you make or encounter in one matter, may require making a change in another.

CABALLO DE BASTOS   CAVALIERE DI BASTONI
RITTER DER STÄBE   CHEVALIER DE BÂTONS

KNIGHT OF WANDS

you be overstressed, or the Knight of Wands appears in reverse, (upside down) treating life with too much contempt, or always having to be the center of attention could bring you more adventure than you can handle.

Although the Knight of Wands does enhance your intuition, it sometimes plays havoc with your timing – which can cause you to lose at time when you expected to win and win at times you thought you'd lose.

The Page of Wands

It's the smaller changes and surprises that can make the biggest difference, in your agenda now. Pages sometimes provide a message concerning pregnancy, children or grandchildren under the age of twenty-five. As a rule, with the Page of Wands, the more reassuring the surrounding cards the better or more welcome the change or news. The less reassuring the surrounding cards the more likely a matter relating to a change in the young persons health, family life, or their companions and personal behavior could become a source of concern.

Children aside, the more encouraging the situation, or other cards in the spread, the easier you will notice and take (or make) small opportunities to blaze your own trail in matters at work and at home. You're likely to receive several small but welcome pieces of good news, invitations or welcome interruptions in your daily routine. This could be the ideal time to take or plan a small "getaway". Should unexpected company arrive, hosting or entertaining them will be more of a pleasure than an ordeal.

The more challenging the situation, or other cards in the spread the harder it may be for you to resist taking petty advantage. A number of last-minute changes from other people could upset your agenda.

Romantically: Should your spread contain a hint of romance, small changes that could

make big differences for the better may be on the horizon in your current relationship or social attitude and environment. **The more reassuring the situation,** or other cards in the spread, accepting an invitation to take a short trip or to attend a small gathering could lead to the discovery that your social skills and power of attraction aren't as rusty as you may have imagined. **The less reassuring the situation,** or other cards in the spread the more you may feel your relationship is changing in small ways that are making you uncomfortable and that you are at a loss to explain.

At your best, you can be child-like, without being childish and you always discover something positive to look forward to.

The Card 26
the Page of Wands

Pages signal small matters with the potential to grow larger – a work in progress.

Key Words:

Changeable/ Surprises

For New Students:

Aside from pregnancy, children and grandchildren, the Page can also signal the figurative "birth" of new ideas and opportunities – or simply a larger number of small inconveniences.

SOTA DE BASTOS
BUBE DER STÄBE

FANTE DI BASTONI
VALET DE BÂTONS

PAGE OF WANDS

However, should you be overstressed, or the Page of Wands appears in reverse, (upside down) you may have to work a little harder than you expected to reach your professional, emotional or academic goals. Instead of "child-like", you may become childish, selfish and manipulative.

Card 26 can enhance your optimism, to assist you in putting matters in perspective, and tying up loose ends – or lend you a little extra spite and malice to keep every-one guessing. Whatever your gender, even the smallest matters now have the potential to become better than you expected or more than you bargained for.

The Ace of Wands

Circumstance, as well as your personal aspirations will force you to blaze your own trail through matters in ways and at times when you least expect it. The more encouraging the situation, or other cards in the spread, the more pleased you'll be by a new turn of events at work or at home. You stand to benefit greatly, whether in the near future or the long run, from changes that begin now even if you are not causing them to happen. Whether you will be offered the opportunity or be forced to make changes in your job, attitude, or behavior, you'll be glad you did. Dramatic changes that might occur in the company you work for could result in a promotion for you or cause you to make a happier and more lucrative job change.

The more challenging the situation, or other cards in the spread the greater the risk of burning yourself out to no avail by trying to force matters to go your way.

Romantically: Should your spread contain a hint of romance, whether or not you are romantically involved at the present time, dramatic changes in your self-awareness will trigger changes in your social habits and behavior that will increase or decrease your emotional availability. **The more reassuring the situation**, or other cards in the spread, an increase in your financial security could revive your desire for companionship, or enable you and your loved on to begin making the best aspects of your relationship, even better. **The less reassuring the situation,** or other cards in the spread, your relationship may prove more vulnerable than you expected to outside pressures from other people's problems. You may surprise others (as well as you) by beginning a relationship that you know is doomed to fail. You or a loved one may suddenly decide to end a relationship, at a time or in a manner, which takes you both by surprise.

At your best, when you choose to harness your willpower with a positive attitude, success can be yours in any area. Just remember, that with any Ace in the Tarot, halfway measures, attitudes and solutions will not be good enough.

Card 27
the Ace of Wands

Aces signify
an inevitable
showdown

Key Words:

Changeable/
Crisis or Reward

For New Students:

The Ace indicates an
approaching break,
or breakthrough in
matters. The better
prepared you are, the
sooner you'll begin
making the most of
your new situation.

However, should you be overstressed, or the Ace of Wands appears in reverse, (upside down) if you are unwilling to accept for whatever mistakes you've made, you could seriously undermine your progress. Sometimes this can also signal the approach of major changes, due to matters beyond your control whether in the natural environment, or among other people and matters at work and home.

Card 27, can trigger sudden changes – in an instant – that can alter the course of your life as well as the lives of other people. However even upsets will be accompanied by a "eureka" moment of crystal clarity, when you realize that you are better off, or better prepared to handle matters than you expected.

The Two of Wands

You'd be wise to be more realistic, than idealistic now. Events that take place at work, at home, or both, will present you with the opportunity to make some changes you'd like to see. Since your instincts for self-preservation are just as strong as your desire to blaze your own trail, the wonders you can accomplish under pressure may surprise you as much as they amaze others. You have the ability to transform dreams into reality. Humility, hard work, humor and honesty are your keys to professional happiness, peace of mind, and accomplishment.

The more encouraging the situation, or other cards in the spread, the more you will have only yourself to thank or blame for changes that you make or refuse to make. Here comes your opening, complete with other people's good will, to prove a point, receive vindication or extricate yourself gracefully from a matter, job or relationship. Your uncanny ability to separate your feelings from the facts in matters can help you make even the most challenging choices and decisions more easily now. However, should your ego, encourage you to climb too high, you can expect to experience a painful fall back into reality.

The more challenging the situation, or other cards in the spread the more you may procrastinate about taking advantage of an opportunity because you doubt your abilities or you encounter more resistance than support from other people. The longer it takes you to develop the necessary patience for untangling fantasy from fact, the longer it may take before you find the personal happiness you deserve. Indecision may cause you to be susceptible to intimidation or manipulation from other people, making it more likely that you will regret not having trusted your own instincts and followed your original plan.

At your best, your ability to remain focused also helps you remain calm and aware of, as well as open to, solutions, opportunities and ideas that other people may miss or ignore. **However, should you be overstressed, or the Two of Wands appears in reverse,** (upside down) you'd be wise to take whatever time

Card 28
the Two of Wands

Subject Card
Two signifies
your attachments.

Keywords:
Changeable/
Attachments

For New Students:

Like the 2ⁿᵈ House
in Astrology, despite
their fondness for
company, our 2's
can also trigger an
awareness of how
much we're recieving
in return from other
people and matters.

is required to get your facts straight before making a decision
or a fuss. If not, you may be too quick to involve yourself and
others in idealistic schemes, based on assumption rather than
fact.

With Card 28 here comes your opening, to prove a point, receive
vindication or gracefully extricate yourself from a matter, job
or relationship, because your level of "attachment" to someone
or something is about to increase or decrease. Whatever the
situation, you will have only yourself to thank or blame for
changes that you make or refuse to make.

The Three of Wands

The greater your concern or anticipation about the future, the more you need to concentrate on handling your current obligations and responsibilities. At this time, you could overcome incredible odds (even emotional or psychological shackles) to reach a particular goal that you may decide was your destiny. Who can say it wasn't? Events at work and home will provide unexpected opportunities for you. You may be able to impart helpful suggestions and ideas that could save the day and bring you positive recognition. At work, home or both, you may be the first person to receive some type of significant news. Personally, professionally (or both) the stronger your ambition the more likely you will notice an increase in your social and professional opportunities. Your ability to communicate effectively with others on a professional or material level may be more in evidence. In personal settings, however, unless you choose your words carefully now, you may create more misunderstandings than you resolve.

The more encouraging the situation, or other cards in the spread, the easier it will be for you say the right thing or provide the correct answer. You are particularly resourceful now – ready and able to accommodate last-minute changes in your own and other people's agendas. You may launch a new idea, concept or theory that will benefit others and enrich your bank account.

The more challenging the situation, or other cards in the spread the more likely you or someone else may let the other down at the last minute, by changing your story or withholding information. You cannot afford to count on last minute rescues or reprieves. The majority of your actions and decisions need to be based on a "do-it-yourself" attitude that will encourage self-reliance.

At your best, you can easily alternate between giving and following orders, depending on which role is more important to your success. **However, should you be overstressed, or the Three of Wands appears in reverse,** (upside down)

Card 29
the Three of Wands

Subject Card
Three is for thinking and networking.

Keywords:

Changeable/ Thinking and Networking

For New Students:
Like the 3ʳᵈ House in Astrology, our 3's also signal news, ideas and activity that keep us in-touch and on our toes, or lead us to change our mind at the last minute.

BASTOS STÄBE   3   BASTONI BÂTONS

WANDS

your talents for making others believe what you say, or your ability to disguise your shortcomings may fail you.

With Card 29 your mindset and moods will have a stronger-than-usual bearing upon how you will absorb and react to whatever is happening around you at home and at work.
You can easily alternate between being a fearless leader and a dedicated follower, depending on which role is more important to your success. You may even impart helpful suggestions and ideas that could save the day and bring you positive recognition.

The Four of Wands

This is all about taking, or creating an opportunity, to construct or complete matters in a manner that is as beneficial to others as it is to you. Events at work and home will provide unexpected opportunities for you make changes that could reinforce your security, by rejuvenate your motivation – if motivation has been a problem for you. Whatever your situation, from finance to romance (and everything in between) the Four of Wands can be one of the most fortunate cards in the Tarot. Since you can master the basics in matters and other people more quickly now, some folks will also be more receptive whatever advice, apologies, or explanations you may offer. Just beware of becoming too sure of yourself or taking too much advantage of situations and other people. Promising more today than you can deliver in the future, as well as hearing and seeing only what you wish in matters now, can be a downside to the Four of Wands.

The more encouraging the situation, or other cards in the spread, the easier it will be for you to orchestrate "happy endings" in matters. Like magic, your dexterity and resilience can enable you to get along more easily, with even the most unusual and difficult people. This may be your chance to discover the truth about your standing in some matters, while preventing or undoing damage in others. Above all, you'll be able to recapture or reinforce your peace of mind.

The more challenging the situation, or other cards in the spread the more likely you are to be your own worst enemy by *not* looking before you leap and *not* thinking before you speak. The harder people try to please you, the more fault you can find with them, and their efforts.

At your best, whatever your situation, by keeping your feet on the ground and viewing matters more realistically, you can attract sound opportunities for advancement in matters at home and work, or even medically and legally. **However,**

Card 30
the Four of Wands

Subject Card
Four is all about your sense of belonging and security.

Keywords:
Changeable/ Belonging and Security

For New Students:

Like the 4th House in Astrology, our 4's, also indicate an increase or decrease in our material and domestic activities, which can strengthen or disturb our sense of belonging and security at work, home or both.

should you be overstressed, or the Four of Wands appears in reverse, (upside down) whatever your situation now, you may soon have good cause to rethink your security. An overabundance of self-involvement, or self-interest may be blinding you to the facts in matters and keeping the happiness you seek just out of reach.

With Card 30 your sense of belonging or desire for security will have a stronger bearing upon matters now. This may be your chance to discover the truth about your standing in some matters, while preventing or undoing damage in others.

The Five of Wands

Here, the Wands desire to blaze their own trail, can become your trial by fire, as unexpected events at work, home (or both) could cause you to question yourself, your work, goals and/or the sincerity of people around you. So, the less time and energy you spend arguing with yourself, the sooner you can regain better control of yourself, matters or both. Whatever the situation, whether it's being fueled by disappointment, provocation or indecision – your biggest opponent is yourself.

The more encouraging the situation, or other cards in the spread, the easier it will be for you to behave honorably, perhaps even volunteering to do more when you'd planned to do less. No matter how upset you may feel about something (or someone), you'll resist the temptation to overstep your bounds. Be glad you did, even if you could get away with misbehaving. Once you're free of whatever emotion you're wrestling with now, you'll be ready and able to accomplish anything. By taking the time to laugh at yourself and matters, you'll find it easier than you expected to make up for whatever time (or money) you may have lost – which may not be as much as you anticipated.

The more challenging the situation, or other cards in the spread the more likely you or other people will make matters harder than they have to be. You may use you're dissatisfaction with one matter as an excuse to start an argument about something else. It may seem impossible to make up your mind. The harder it is for you to get along with yourself, the harder it will be for others' to get along with you.

At your best, the better you feel about you, the greater your physical and mental energy will be. Thus the less likely you are to incur any permanent setbacks, or lose anything you cannot live more easily without. **However, should you be overstressed, or the Five of Wands appears in reverse,** (upside down) should it seem as if the

Card 31
the Five of Wands

Subject Card Five is a card of conflict and speculation.

Keywords:

Changeable/ Conflict and Speculation

For New Students:
Like the 5th House in Astrology, our 5's can also trigger an unexpected conflict of interest between our logic and emotions, in matters ranging from duty, to friendship,finance, romance - or parenting.

moment you rid yourself of one problem you're confronting another, perhaps your insistence upon burning yourself out in no-win situations could be why you can neither relax nor get ahead.

With Card 31, since accepting or initiating change may not come easily the more confidently you express yourself, the less likely other people will be to challenge you. The harder it is for you to get along with yourself, the harder it will be for others to get along with you.

The Six of Wands

This is all about teamwork! So, here's to "Victory"— with the help of friends!" As long as you're comfortable with, and confident about your endeavor, you're sure to attract or recruit the best people or partners. Events at work and at home will provide unexpected opportunities for you to demonstrate your leadership, friendship, loyalty and cooperation. Taking proper advantage of these opportunities could boost your self-esteem and your status. Since the Six of Wands is an auspicious card it can suddenly bring you into contact with people who are in a position to assist you or advance your interests, which can be especially favorable for those with professional or political aspirations.

The more encouraging the situation, or other cards in the spread, the easier you can achieve any number of victories with, or for other people at work and at home. Enlisting and extending assistance will help make everyone's agenda easier and more enjoyable. Should circumstances force you to co-operate with, or contact someone you're uncomfortable with, or who is uncomfortable with you, you might discover you have more in common than you thought. You may be called upon to negotiate a truce between opposing factions at work or home. Socially, this is an ideal time to take advantage of any opportunities to join positive club or group endeavors. This is the right time to meet new people and solidify existing relationships. No matter where you are, you may have a better time than you expected.

The more challenging the situation, or other cards in the spread, whatever your situation you're more likely to resist offers of assistance or advice and suggestions that could improve matters for you. No matter where you go, or whom you're with you're less likely to enjoy yourself as much as you'd hoped.

At your best, you instinctively know how and when to attract an audience and hold their attention. You enjoy

Card 32
the Six of Wands

Subject Card Six represents commitment.

Keywords:

Changeable / Commitment

For New Students:
Like the 6th House in Astrology, our 6's also signal situations and opportunities that can enhance or disrupt our personal peace of mind, as we strive to keep pace with matters and people that comprise our daily routine.

helping others and you welcome friendly competition. **However, should you be overstressed, or the Six of Wands appears in reverse,** (upside down) you can turn your charisma on and off like a faucet. Any gains that you may be anticipating, will either be delayed, or not as large as you expected.

With Card 32 you can be the perfect partner or team player – as willing to teach other people, as you are ready to learn from them, by simply refreshing your perspective. However, the more certain you are of others loyalty, favor or affection the more you need to beware taking them for granted.

The Seven of Wands

This is all about your adaptability! The more adaptable you are, the more you stand to gain – the less adaptable you are, the longer you'll have to contend with upsetting circumstances. Thanks to the unique mix of opportunities and obstacles that karma and circumstance are about to toss into your path, you're going to need a little more persistence to reach your goals – no matter how simple or complex they may be. The good news is that your sense of humor and fair play can provide an unbeatable advantage by lending you whatever extra patience and energy you may need. Replenishing your energies through optimism and faith, can prevent pessimism from spoiling your mood as well as, whatever you hope to promote.

The more encouraging the situation, or other cards in the spread, the more your advice or assistance will be required It may be necessary to rearrange your agenda and reconsider your priorities. A soothing manner can make it virtually impossible for others to remain in a bad mood in your company, enabling you to achieve a mutual understanding more easily. Taking a direct yet non-threatening approach will inspire others to try and work harder or correct their mistakes, without feeling that you are pushing or judging them.

The more challenging the situation, or other cards in the spread the more likely you are to feel as if you can't please anyone, no matter how you try. Although you may consider yourself the victim, you may be the perpetrator of your own unhappiness, by refusing to abandon thought patterns and habits that are doing you more harm than good. Knowing when to throw away psychological and emotional crutches and doing it are two different matters.

Card 33
the Seven of Wands

Subject Card Seven corresponds to your relationships.

Keywords:

Changeable/ Relationships

For New Students:
Like the 7th House in Astrology, our 7's can also signal an unexpected turn of events - for better or worse, concerning our relationships, at work, home or both.

At your best: you can bring matters out in the open in a manner that offends no-one and benefits everyone.

However, should you be overstressed, or the Seven of Wands appears in reverse, (upside down) perhaps you've been taking your frustrations out on others without realizing it. Then again, you may not be as adaptable as you imagine. Either way, you may need to reconsider your position.

Card 33 can enable you to make beneficial changes in your relationships.

The Eight of Wands

Expect the unexpected in yourself, matters and people now. Anytime the Eight of Wands appears, very few matters will follow prescribed guidelines and rules. No matter how certain you are of where you're going and what you're doing, whether by choice or necessity, you're about to take a step back from matters you're working on to adjust the accuracy of your focus. At work or home, unexpected events at work and home can instigate the need to move more quickly to complete, salvage or launch current matters in order to accommodate new matters. You may need to take an unplanned trip, or devise a new route or method of travel in your daily routine.

The more encouraging the situation, or other cards in the spread, the more you can accomplish in less time than you expected. Necessity is the mother of invention and you will be at your innovative best, making sound decisions more quickly than usual. Socially, professionally (or both) you may become an overnight success or sensation. One or more pieces of good news could leave you feeling better and more confident (or desirable) than you have in some time.

The more challenging the situation, or other cards in the spread, you may suddenly feel as if matters are running away with you and over you, making it harder to absorb everything that's happening. Perhaps you've never mastered your temper. Perhaps you're simply too quick to imagine the worst. Whatever your concerns, the less certain you are of where you're going in life the sooner you realize it's you, that must change, the sooner you can transform your behavior and attitude from becoming part of the problem, into part of the solution.

At your best, your opportunistic nature, positive attitude and bold maneuvers can insure your success. **However,**

Card 34
the Eight of Wands

Subject Card Eight stands for future renovation.

Keywords:
Changeable/ Renovation

For New Students: Like the 8th House in Astrology, our 8's often provides clues concerning the stability of our future, with anyone or anything that is important to us.

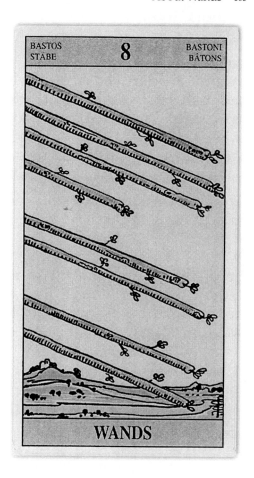

should you be overstressed, or the Eight of Wands appears in reverse, (upside down) whether or not you'd been expecting them to, matters may begin moving more quickly than you are prepared to deal with. The harder you've tried to believe that happy endings create themselves, the more disappointed you may be.

Card 34 can enable you to deal more quickly, logically, and effectively with multiple opportunities and situations that could stabilize or change matters for the better.

The Nine of Wands

The Nine of Wands is all about victory – after a struggle. Unexpected events at work and home could tax your physical stamina. Whether you've encountered a number of minor set-backs, close calls or taken a few hard falls in recent matters, it's time to reassess your values and change the habits that brought you to this impasse. The Nine of Wands is not a quitter, nor should you be. It simply bears out the old adage that everything happens for a reason.

The more encouraging the situation, or other cards in the spread, the easier you can grasp the positive essence of whatever lessons you've learned, or are learning. Whatever the situation, your new outlook can enhance the practicality of your thinking, enabling your emotions to begin working for (rather than against) whatever you hope to achieve. Whether you are hoping to make a comeback or a debut, taking matters one step at a time and trying not to look or plan too far ahead will aid you in replenishing your confidence and energy as you begin to move forward.

The more challenging the situation, or other cards in the spread the harder it may be for you to make the changes that you know you need to make. You may be in danger of falling back into habits, attitudes and situations that could hamper your advancement. Depression can trigger a disconnection between your emotions and reality.

At your best, each victory you score against pessimism and procrastination transforms one more stumbling block into a stepping-stone that brings you closer to achieving your goals. **However, should you be overstressed,** or the Nine of Wands appears in reverse, (upside down) the greater your sense of loss or confusion, the more distance you may put between your feelings and the facts. Whatever your situation, you'd be especially wise to rethink

Card 35
the Nine of Wands

Subject Card
**Nine represents
your understanding.**

Keywords:
**Changeable/
Understanding**

For New Students:
Like the 9th House
in Astrology, our 9's
can make it easier
or more challenging
to expand our out-
look while maintain-
ing our beliefs and
self-confidence.

matters before making any changes now. You probably
have more options than you're willing to consider.

With Card 35 you always gain something of value from
your experiences once you learn to relax and go with the
flow, even when the tide seems to be against you. Whatever you learn or discover now, can be the catalyst that
inspires you to try harder, try again or seek a better direction. "When you change the way you look at things, the
things you look at change."

The Ten of Wands

It's all about endurance. Whatever the situation, you're at a crossroads concerning your ability to absorb and work with any additional stress and tension. Situations at work and at home will provide you with opportunities to make changes that can redirect the course of your life for the better – if you're not afraid to try. For whatever reason, the life-or-death intensity that you have attached to matters is transforming your powers of endurance into more of a hang-up than an advantage.

The more encouraging the situation, or other cards in the spread, the more you will welcome, and work with, the chance to make changes that can improve the way you think, work or feel. The more positive your attitude the easier you can remain focused on the more positive aspects in matters and make the impossible possible, when you least expect it. From jobs to relationships, the better your reasons for letting go, the sooner you can find something better, whether or not you've been looking.

The more challenging the situation, or other cards in the spread the easier you can devise excuses for remaining in the same old rut and breaking promises you've made to other people and yourself. The more cynical or apprehensive your attitude, the more often you will misconstrue the facts and create more problems in your mind, than really exist in the matters at hand. The more you doubt yourself the more defensive you may be of whatever illusion you have created.

At your best, by remaining focused on what you really want to do, be or have, you can avoid feeling disheartened or blowing smaller issues out of proportion. **However, should you be overstressed,** or the Ten of Wands appears in reverse, (upside down) feeling or believing

Card 36
the Ten of Wands

Subject Card
Ten represents
Achievement.

Keywords:
**Changeable/
Achievement**

For New Students:
Like the 10th House
in Astrology, since
our 10's can lead us
to feel as if we're
closer too or farther
away from achiev-
ing our goals, they
can also make
whatever we're
doing more or less
enjoyable.

that you are doomed to carry the weight of the world on your shoulders could start to become a bad habit. Perhaps you are the only one that is expecting too much out of yourself.

Although Card 36 tends to heighten your desire and ability to accommodate others, it can also weaken your ability, whether to believe in yourself or to know what you really want, or want to do for yourself.

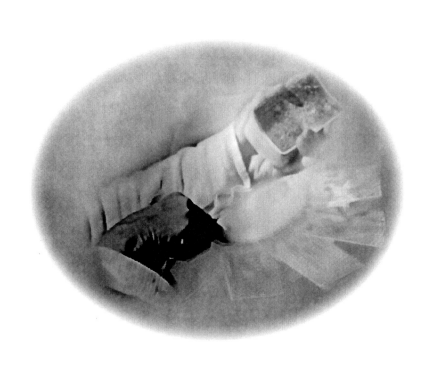

ABOUT CUPS[1]

Keyword: Emotion

Element: Water

Corresponding Astrological Signs: Cancer ♋, Scorpio ♏ and Pisces ♓.

Corresponding Playing Card: Hearts.

Function: Cups can enable you to keep maters flowing at an easy pace, or freeze everything in its tracks.

---

[1] aka. Goblets, Chalices, Hearts, Teacups, Gourds, etc. in some Tarot Decks.

CHAPTER 4

In Tarot, the element of Water corresponds to the suit of Cups as well as the Astrological Water Signs, Cancer ♋, Scorpio ♏ and Pisces ♓. Water is the most engaging and chameleon-like of all the elements, just like your personal hopes and dreams. So, whether you're seeking to absorb or initiate change Cups can enable you to keep maters flowing at an easy pace, or freeze everything in its' tracks, or appear as if you are taking a very rational approach to matters, even when you aren't. Just as water supports all forms of physical life, Cups symbolize everything that adds meaning to YOUR life. They are the strongest of all the suits in the Minor Arcana because they prompt your intuition and promote the motions that nourish your behavior and dreams. However, should you be over-stressed Cups can warn you against becoming too needy or depressed, anytime your feelings are in danger of over-riding your commonsense.

The more encouraging the situation, the more logically you can deal with your feelings, share them and rely on their accuracy. The more challenging the situation the easier and more quickly your emotions could impel you to begin or purse matters that you'd be wiser and better off, to leave alone. Should Cups comprise the majority of your spread the matters at hand may prove to be more complex than they appear, or your manner of handling them may be more emotional than the matter itself. The more quickly you make up your mind, the harder it may be to follow the course of action you resolve to take.

KEY POINTS WHEN READING CUPS

All Cups correlate to the Astrological Water Signs, Cancer ♋, Scorpio ♏ and Pisces ♓

"Emotion (al)" implies that you are, or will be, seeking to absorb or initiate an experience that could stabilize or unsettle your personal comfort zone.

Cups can enable you to keep matters flowing at an easy pace, or freeze everything in its' tracks.

Cups represent emotional sensitivity and intuition.

Cups symbolize everything that adds meaning to your life.

Cups can enable you to deal with your feelings more logically, share them and rely on their accuracy.

However, under more stressful conditions, Cups can also warn you against becoming too needy, depressed or allowing your feelings to override your commonsense.

Subject Cards 2-10 often signify situations, advantages, opportunities, moods or obstacles that come out of nowhere, and sometimes pass just as quickly.

THE CUPS

The King of Cups

The King of Cups lends you the cunning of a Scorpio, the obscurity of a Pisces and the sense of duty of a Cancer, to provide you with a truly unique approach to obtaining your objectives and frustrating your adversaries. When necessary, your chameleon-like ability to camouflage yourself and matters can enable you to zoom to the top in every instance, no matter how far down you may have started or allowed yourself to be pushed. **The more encouraging the situation,** or the other cards in the spread, the more it will seem that you can accomplish by doing less. Many matters will seem to fall into place just as you'd hoped, and apparently of their own accord. Meetings or interviews with authority figures are likely to go quite smoothly as you can direct the flow along any path you choose. At work and at home people seem to anticipate your wishes willingly comply with any special requests you may have. The happier you are, the happier everyone around you seems to be. You may contact or be contacted by people at a distance bearing good news related to your personal or professional affairs.

The more challenging the situation, or the other cards in the spread the less willing people will be to comply with your agenda. The harder you try to regain control of matters the more control seems to elude you. Meetings or interviews with authority figures, as well as personal plans or conversations with friends and family are likely to prove counterproductive.

Romantically: Should your spread contain a hint of romance, you may begin to realize that you've been alone too long, or that you care more deeply for someone than you were aware of. **The more reassuring the situation**, or other cards in the spread, the more likely the attraction will be mutual. **The less reassuring the situation**, or other cards in the spread the more complex and possibly less rewarding your relationship will be.

Card 37
the King of Cups

Kings trigger or enhance your initiative.

Keywords:
Emotional/ Initiative

For New Students: Whatever your gender or situation, the King can enable you to set new wheels in motion, or handle on-going situations more effectively – whether to gain an upper hand in matters or mount a solid defense.

REY DE COPAS   RE DI COPPE
KÖNIG DER KELCHE   ROI DE COUPES

KING OF CUPS

At your best, your positive character, shrewd judgment and natural caring enable you to tackle your responsibilities with an open mind and a sense of fun, almost as if you were planning a picnic. **However, should you be overstressed,** or Card 37 the King of Cups appears in reverse, (upside down) your initiative may be lacking in sincerity, and it may be as easy for you to lie to yourself as to other people.

Card 37 intensifies your desire and ability to impress, improve, preserve, defend or even destroy whatever (or whoever) you feel to be yours, depending upon your mood at the moment.

The Queen of Cups

At work and home, you can choose to be the catalyst for harmony, or disharmony. You are very analytical, (sometimes even calculating) and you don't like losing. Your ability to set and follow a separate (not necessarily) secret agenda can help you retain your objectivity and prevent problems from overwhelming you. Although you often draw new strength from opposition, your ability to camouflage yourself and blend in with people and situations, whenever you feel uncertain, can sometimes be your guardian angel.

The more encouraging the situation, or other cards in the spread, the more inspirational your example will prove to be. At work and at home you can please and charm everyone with a smile or a glance. You emit a positive yet soothing effect that makes everyone feel more alive and confident. Without even trying, you can breathe new life and hope into dead issues, solve perplexing problems and settle quarrels to everyone's satisfaction. People who can further your interests seem to appear out of nowhere – ready to oblige. **The more challenging the situation,** or other cards in the spread the more you could use your influence and impact to deliberately spoil or delay matters for other people. The harder you try to mask your irritability, or unhappiness, the more obvious and contagious it becomes.

Romantically: Should your spread contain a hint of romance, you could soon meet the love of your life, or begin an infatuation that controls your life. The more reassuring the situation or other cards in the spread, romance may change your entire approach to life with positive results. The less reassuring the situation or the other cards in the spread the more disruptive your relationship may be.

At your best, your no-nonsense behavior is coupled with a caring attitude. You never rely on one matter or person to be your answer to everything. You enjoy people who are not afraid to be themselves. **However, should you be overstressed,** or the Queen of Cups appears in reverse, (upside down) your

Card 38
the Queen of Cups

Queens can
enhance your people
and coping skills.

Keywords:
Emotional/ Charm

For New Students:

Whatever your
gender or situation,
the Queen can enable
you to keep everyone
and everything "on
the same page," more
easily, by managing
people and cultivating
matters with greater
efficiency.

REINA DE COPAS   REGINA DI COPPE
KÖNIGIN DER KELCHE   REINE DE COUPES

QUEEN OF CUPS

diversity may cause others' to feel you're not taking your
commitments seriously. You may require some time alone to
refresh your perspective and inner self, particularly if it seems
that self-interest is beginning to undermine your charisma.

Card 38 will awaken or enhance your ability to obtain or
retain control of situations and people that are essential to
your ongoing stability. Whatever your gender, your people
and coping skills are about to be tested or required.

The Knight of Cups

The greater your determination to succeed, the more likely you win your objective through a combination of hard work, and incredibly smooth moves. All Knights are reactionaries. Each Knight has the potential to stimulate a different type of personal behavior, and the Knight of Cups can lend you just the right amount of psychological subtlety to outwit an opponent or win your hearts desire.

The more encouraging the situation, or other cards in the spread, the greater your willingness to let bygones be bygones and tackle matters that you normally dislike with a cheery attitude. Your humorous approach to matters that interrupt your agenda enables you to maintain your schedule. A number of pleasant social invitations or professional proposals could come your way – like magic. You're particularly intuitive now and your dreams may be more precognitive.

The more challenging the situation, or other cards in the spread the more challenging it may be to talk your way out of any matters you've mishandled. The more charming, or agreeable you try to be, the less impressed and more annoyed other people seem to be. At work and at home matters that were going well may begin to disintegrate before your eyes with no explanation. Travel or social plans could change or fall through at the last minute.

Romantically: Should your spread contain a hint of romance, **The more reassuring the situation**, or other cards in spread, the more likely it is that you could fall in love more quickly than you expected or intended. **The less reassuring the situation**, or other cards in the spread the more likely it is that you, or the object of your affection are not being completely honest with one another.

At your best, your ability to understand others so well, stems from your willingness to be honest with others and learn from your past mistakes. When possible, you prefer coercing your opponents to challenging them. **However, should you be overstressed**, or the Knight of Cups appears

Card 39
the Knight of Cups

Knights indicate unexpected developments in matters or your behavior.

Keywords:

Emotional/ Adventure

For New Students:

Since Knights produce a "domino' effect, whether it's more expedient to move forward or step back for now, any changes you make or encounter in one matter may require making a change in another.

CABALLO DE COPAS   CAVALIERE DI COPPE
RITTER DER KELCHE   CHEVALIER DE COUPES

KNIGHT OF CUPS

in reverse, (upside down) there may be very little sincerity behind your promises, or any depth to the affection you claim to possess. Whatever the situation, beware the temptation to lull yourself into a false sense of security.

Although Card 39 lends you diplomacy, coupled with an instinctual knowledge of the psychological subtleties that motivate other people, your talent for promoting unity in some matters is equally balanced against your skill for sowing the seeds of dissension in others.

The Page of Cups

The Page of Cups signals an inevitable turning point where one or more matters that have gone on so long in one direction will begin to change course – for better or worse. Pages sometimes provide a message concerning pregnancy, children or grandchildren under the age of twenty five. As a rule, with the Page of Cups, the more reassuring the surrounding cards the less surprising the change or news. Whatever transpires, may even confirm a "premonition" that you've had. The less reassuring the surrounding cards the more likely a matter relating to the young persons health, family life, or their social development and personal behavior could become a source of greater interest, concern or both.

Children aside, the more encouraging the situation, or other cards in the spread, the easier it will be for you to address and express your feelings rather than deny them. At work and at home you'll become more aware of how much and why you like or dislike certain people and matters. You'll feel more self-confident about handling matters you've been avoiding. You may be more receptive to the idea of becoming pregnant or considering adoption, seeking better employment, or beginning a new hobby, whether as a means of broadening your social horizons or some much needed personal relaxation. **The more challenging the situation,** or other cards in the spread the harder it may be to resist delivering or responding to ultimatums that could do more harm than good. Problems in your emotional life could begin to affect your professional life, or professional problems could begin to unbalancing matters in your personal life. Smaller annoyances or disagreements could rapidly and mysteriously escalate into full-fledged confrontations. Family turmoil could bring the news of (or the responsibility for) a "little someone" that you didn't expect at your door.

Romantically: Should your spread contain a hint of romance, you'll discover that your feelings for someone are changing. **The more reassuring the situation**, or other cards in spread, the more likely you could feel that a friendship is capable of becoming more. You may feel as if you're starting to fall in love all over again with your current mate or partner. You may become more interested in meeting new people socially. **The**

Card 40
the Page of Cups

Pages signal small matters with the potential to grow larger – a work in progress.

Keywords:

Emotional/ Surprises

For New Students:

Aside from pregnancy, children and grandchildren, the Page can also signal the figurative "birth" of new ideas, and opportunities – or simply a larger number of small inconveniences.

SOTA DE COPAS   FANTE DI COPPE
BUBE DER KELCHE   VALET DE COUPES

PAGE OF CUPS

less reassuring the situation, or other cards in the spread the more you may feel as if continuing your present relationship would be a mistake.

At your best, you can be forthright without being too forward. You can be a good listener, and your ability to discern truth from falsehood can enable you to stay one step ahead in matters. **However, should you be overstressed,** or the Page of Cups appears in reverse, (upside down) a tendency to exaggerate, fostered by the desire to appear more important or knowledgeable than you are, will only create fresh problems.

Card 40 can either assist you in re-evaluating matters with more honesty and less idealism, or in mistaking desire for destiny.

The Ace of Cups

Whatever, your situation, by working more constructively with your emotions now, you can make this time period more productive and rewarding. **The more encouraging the situation,** or other cards in the spread, the more grateful, relieved or thankful you'll feel about a new turn of events at work or at home. You may feel as if a cloud or burden that you've been laboring under has been lifted. You'll feel more charitable and understanding towards other people. You may even be more creative or outgoing than ever before. Your premonitions and dreams could be uncommonly strong – and accurate. Keeping an open heart and mind, can help prevent your emotions from getting the better of your commonsense. Retaining some degree of personal freedom to express as well as experience your emotions is essential to achieving a harmonious blend and balance between your emotions and behavior.

The more challenging the situation, or other cards in the spread the greater the risk of making matters worse or borrowing additional trouble by trying to force things to go your way. You may be too emotional to see matters clearly.

Romantically: Should your spread contain a hint of romance, it may be virtually impossible to keep your feelings to yourself. **The more reassuring the situation,** or other cards in spread, the more likely you may receive or deliver a proposal of marriage or passionate declaration of love. You could renew your marriage vows, surprise or be surprised by an overwhelmingly romantic gift or gesture. You may soon become a willing victim of love-at-first-sight. **The less reassuring the situation,** or other cards in the spread the more likely you and/or your loved one are to have a bitter and hurtful quarrel. You may feel as if you're being overwhelmed emotionally.

At your best, you don't have to pin down exactly where your feelings come from every moment. Your emotions help you enhance – not escape the reality of life. Your contagious and inspirational zest for life may encourage you to accomplish feats that leave others in awe. **However, should you be overstressed,** or the Ace of Cups appears in reverse, (upside down)

Card 41
the Ace of Cups

Aces signify an inevitable showdown

Keywords:

Emotional/ Crisis or Reward

For New Students:

The Ace indicates an approaching break, or breakthrough in matters. The better prepared you are, the sooner you'll begin making the most of your new situation.

the more challenging it can be to come to grips with your emotions as well as any emotional negativity that you encounter. The stronger your cynicism or self-pity the more jealous, possessive or self-indulgent you can become.

With Card 41, you're likely to experience one or more feelings that are as unusual, or new to you, as the experiences they reach you through. Yet, even upsets will be accompanied by a moment of crystal clarity, when you realize that you are better off, or better equipped to handle matters than you expected.

The Two of Cups

Whatever the situation, your feelings can enable you to be a more formidable opponent or powerful ally than either you or other people may expect. Events that take place at work, at home, or both, will strengthen your affection and loyalty, or suspicion and irritation with people. **The more encouraging the situation,** or other cards in the spread, the easier it will be for you and other people to understand and relate to one another harmoniously. At work, home or both, you can combine your organizational abilities and people skills more effectively than ever. Even the most reticent people will feel more confident, positive and alive in your company. You'll feel less threatened by other people's independence, less hesitant to exercise your own initiative. You'll also be more receptive to any good suggestions or advice. The more supportive you are of other peoples' endeavors, the more willingly they'll endorse your projects. The good impressions you make reflect how good you feel.

The more challenging the situation, or other cards in the spread the more you may feel as if everyone is against you or trying to patronize you. Your feelings of irritation or uncertainty could contaminate even the jolliest atmosphere at work and at home – causing everyone to feel uneasy.

Romantically: The more reassuring the situation, or other cards in spread, the greater your social opportunities for romantic possibilities. Sharing hobbies and interests with your mate or partner can make you a "perfect party of two." **The less reassuring the situation,** or other cards in the spread the more likely it is that you and the object of your affection will disagree about a particular matter or course of action.

At Your Best, you're as attracted to positive people and endeavors as they are to you. Your ability to simultaneously strike the right chord with some people, while hitting the wrong note with others, can lend a note of sparkling controversy to your popularity.

**Card 42
the Two of Cups**

Subject Card Two
signifies your
attachments.

Keywords:
**Changeable/
Attachments**

For New Students:
Like the 2nd House in
Astrology, despite its
fondness for company,
our 2's also trigger
an awareness of how
much we're recieving
in return from other
people and matters.

However, should you be overstressed, or the Two of Cups
appears in reverse, (upside down) whatever the situation,
matters and people you thought you couldn't get along without,
may suddenly annoy you to no end. You'd be especially wise
to avoid people and entertainments that bring out your worst
– instead of your best traits.

Card 42 activates your desire for company, acceptance and
security - sometimes to the point of overstimulation, which can
undermine your better judgment.

The Three of Cups

This is all about sharing. At work and home all sorts of gossip, as well as a few nuggets of pertinent information will soon be traveling your way. Events at work and home will provide ample opportunities for you and other people to express and discuss your feelings. You are fueled by the determination to find a better way, or a better answer as well as a need to know, see and do as much as possible. Whatever the situation, your desire to share and process ideas and information can make it easier to develop new approaches and techniques concerning matters from finance to romance and everything in between

The more encouraging the situation, or other cards in the spread, the easier it will be to resolve any potential or genuine misunderstandings. You'll feel particularly communicative now, ready to listen with an open mind and respond with sincerity, clarity and diplomacy. People "in the know" are inclined to share information and take the time to listen and talk with you. You may reach a decision or receive news that deserves a night on the town or a weekend getaway. You may host or attend a gathering or even become the recipient of an award, prize or trip.

The more challenging the situation, or other cards in the spread the more carefully you should check your timing and your facts before believing or disbelieving anything you hear and especially what you feel.

Romantically: The more reassuring the situation, or other cards in spread, the more likely you could meet someone special, perhaps through a friend whether by accident or prearrangement. **The less reassuring the situation,** or other cards in the spread the more likely you and the object of your affection may try to incite each other's jealousy – perhaps without realizing it.

At your best, by listening to or sympathizing with everyone, but siding with no one you can remain in everyones good graces, without becoming anyone's fool. You always have a positive argument that can transform virtually any procrastinator into a willing participant. Others can rely on you to your word and

Card 43
the Three of Cups

Subject Card Three is for thinking and networking.

Keywords:

Emotional/ Thinking and Networking

For New Students:

Like the 3rd House in Astrology, our 3's also signal news, ideas and activity that can keep us in-touch and on-our-toes, or lead us to change our mind at the last minute.

their secrets. **However, should you be overstressed**, or the Three of Cups appears in reverse (upside down) someone close to you may be guilty of embellishing the truth, or failing to keep a secret. Whatever the situation, your imagination may lead you to believe that other people are fighting over you—or with you, or that someone else is the only cause or answer to your dilemma.

Card 43 is 43 is seldom without an agenda when acquiring or delivering information.

Four of Cups

It's all about taking "a leap of faith" whether in you, other people, matters or all three. Events at work and at home will trigger feelings of anxiety or self-satisfaction relating to people and matters you feel are necessary for your well-being. Whatever the situation, you are being stimulated by a unique blend of material and emotional elements. So whether or not you're more intuitive now, you're definitely more aware of possibilities and pitfalls that others either can't or won't see, which could enable you to defuse potential problems and plan ahead more easily.

The more encouraging the situation, or other cards in the spread, the happier you'll feel about your job, material security and your role in your relationships. A number of pleasant possibilities for increasing your material security and emotional satisfaction are within your grasp. The greater your desire to move forward in life, the easier you can devise a more effective course of action that will enhance your resourcefulness, spirituality and creativity.

  The more challenging the situation, or other cards in the spread the more uncertain you may feel about present and the future. You may question the wisdom of your recent choices or behavior. This is not a good time to concoct believable excuses. Avoid the temptation to get carried away by feelings of "would-have, should-have, and could-have". They will make it more challenging to untangle your feelings.

Romantically: The more reassuring the situation, or other cards in the spread, the easier you can stop living in the past or avoid repeating your past mistakes. The less reassuring the situation or the other cards in the spread the harder it may be to put your past disappointments behind you, and believe that the best is yet to come – although it is.

At your best, you won't allow others' insecurities to influence your decisions. Being in touch with your "higher self" lends you the courage to follow what "feels right" to you, whether or not everyone else approves or understands. **However, should you be overstressed,** or the Four of Cups appears in reverse,

Card 44
Four of Cups

Subject Card Four is all about your sense of belonging and security.

Keywords:

Emotional/ Belonging and Security

For New Students:

Like the 4th House in Astrology, our 4's signal an increase or decrease in our material and domestic activities, that can strengthen or disturb our sense of belonging and security.

(upside down) some of you may feel it's impossible for you to relax, or seek (and follow) even the most reliable advice or medical assistance until either your work is done or your dilemma resolved. Others may be in denial, or taking too much for granted – whether by refusing to believe matters could change, or refusing to accept they have changed.

Although Card 44 can sharpen or awaken your intuition, whether or not your intuitive promptings can clarify matters depends upon your willingness to work with the truths you uncover.

The Five of Cups

Whatever the situation, your awareness of the past does not have to keep you chained to it. Events at work and at home could cause you to question yourself, your work, goals or the sincerity of people around you. Encouraging yourself to take more satisfaction in the present, and be happy with who you are will bolster your self-confidence about the future.

The more encouraging the situation, or other cards in the spread, the easier you can avoid melancholy by giving yourself something positive to look forward to. This is especially important if you're grappling with a recent setback or emotional disappointment. The more you give yourself to look forward to, the easier you can keep the past in perspective and confront the present. The more diversified your interests, the easier you can keep moving forward.

The more challenging the situation, or other cards in the spread developing a "what's-the-use" attitude or behavior will only increase your worry. The more you believe you can do for other people, the more you'll realize they must do for themselves. The more you expect other people to do for you, the more you'll have to do for yourself. The sooner you accept any disturbing premonitions or dreams that you might have, as an "early warning system" the sooner you conquer any anxiety they may cause you. Talking with a friend or perhaps a professional counselor could help.

Romantically: The more reassuring the situation, or other cards in the spread, the easier it may be to resolve an emotional misunderstanding or achieve a mutual parting. The less reassuring the situation or other cards in spread, the more important it is that you don't backslide into self-defeating habits or relationships. Talking with a friend or perhaps a professional counselor could help.

At your best, you're reflective, resourceful and conscientious about "reaping what you sow." **However, should you be overstressed,** or the Five of Cups appears in reverse, (upside down), expecting the worst only sets you up

Card 45
the Five of Cups

Subject Card Five is a card of conflict and speculation.

Keywords:

Emotional/ Conflict and Speculation

For New Students:
Like the 5th House in Astrology, our 5's can also trigger an unexpected conflict of interest between our logic and emotions, in matters ranging from duty, to friendship, finance, romance -or parenting.

for your next disappointment and makes it easier to did yourself deeper into matters and moods you've been trying to get out of. You'd also be wise to beware becoming involved (or re-involved) with people, matters or habits that will only disappoint you.

With Card 45, the less you believe that you can handle without assistance, the greater your surprise at how much smoother matters flow when you do handle them alone.

The Six of Cups

It's all about taking a closer look at how far you've come, and counting your blessings. Some events at work and at home may provide overdue vindication, or perhaps an opportunity to receive or express heartfelt appreciation. Other events may trigger feelings of nostalgia. Good deeds you've done in the past, that seemed to go unnoticed, could bear fruit now. Whatever your situation, you're likely to encounter one or more inexplicable episodes of deja'vu, pre-cognitive dreams or eerily accurate hunches.

The more encouraging the situation, or other cards in the spread, the more likely you are to hear something from, or about, someone from your past. You may meet someone, or travel to someplace that "feels" familiar to you although you've never seen them before now. Avenues and opportunities that were closed are beginning to open.

The more challenging the situation, or the other cards in the spread the more likely a past indiscretion or oversight or possibly a medical issue could resurface, to your disadvantage.

Romantically: the more reassuring the situation, or other cards in the spread, the more likely your relationship could be changing for the better. You may resume a former relationship. You may receive an opportunity to date someone you've been interested in for a while; or you may give someone a chance to date you. **The less reassuring the situation**, or other cards in spread, the more likely you are to wonder if what you have to show in your social life or in your relationship is really worth everything you've put yourself through to maintain it.

At your best: knowing that you are doing the best you can – in the best way possible will refresh your faith and strengthen your ability to keep working towards a brighter

Card 46
the Six of Cups

Subject Card Six
represents commitment.

Keywords:

Emotional/
Commitment

For New Students:

Like the 6th House in Astrology, our 6's can also signal situations that can enhance or disrupt our peace of mind as we strive to keep pace with matters and people that comprise our daily routine.

tomorrow. **However, should you be overstressed,** or the Six of Cups appears in reverse, (upside down), you may soon be contacted by, or have cause to contact, someone you'd been hoping to avoid. The greater your preoccupation with the more negative elements of your past and present, the less you need to wonder why your future appears so bleak. Talking with a friend, religious advisor or professional counselor could help.

With Card 46, unbidden thoughts and memories from your past will play small but significant roles in the manner you handle your present concerns and chart your future.

The Seven of Cups

You're about to discover that you've over or underestimated someone - or something, for better or worse. Events at work and at home may prompt you to re-evaluate one or more of your relationships – for better or worse, or one matter going askew could put your entire agenda "up in the air" – for better or worse.

The more encouraging the situation, or other cards in the spread, the easier it will be to rearrange matters in order of their importance. You may be pleasantly surprised to discover that you have more free time than you expected.

The more challenging the situation, or other cards in the spread the more likely it is that you'll have to make apologies, or excuses, or even substitute for someone at work, at home, or both. Your talent for making matters appear to be as you wish they were could convince everyone that you're telling the truth - when nothing could be farther from the truth. The longer you deny issues you don't want to confront, the harder it will be to remain focused on the matters you do enjoy.

Romantically: The more reassuring the situation, or other cards in the spread, the more likely it is that you'll discover you have more social and romantic options than you had imagined. Your social adaptability and versatility make you a welcome addition to any gathering. **The less reassuring the situation,** or other cards in spread, the more likely it is that you could make two dates for the same day without realizing it! Something you've heard, or seen, or said and done, may raise questions or doubts that need to be addressed now.

At your best: the more practical and realistic you are, the easier and more likely you are to transform losing matters into winning propositions – much to the consternation of your adversaries, and the delight of your supporters.

Card 47
the Seven of Cups

Subject Card Seven corresponds to relationships.

Keywords:
Emotional/ Relationships

For New Students:
Like the 7th House in Astrology, our 7's can also signal an unexpected turn of events – for better or worse, concerning our relationships, at work, home or both.

However, should you be overstressed, or the Seven of Cups appears in reverse, (upside down) your insistence on putting "too many irons in the fire" could cost you more than if you'd taken the time to handle matters more realistically. Circumstances may soon cause you to feel as if you're running a day late and a dollar short!

For better or worse, Card 47 can enable you to become a combination of actor and a miracle worker – by transforming you into a master – or mistress of illusion.

The Eight of Cups

Whatever your situation, administering a personal reality check can help refresh and maintain your inner balance and clarity of purpose. Card 48 can symbolize emotional transformation, or a spiritual reawakening – and sometimes both. This is the individualist.

The more encouraging the situation, or other cards in the spread, the easier it will be for you to resolve conflicting emotions that have been undermining your individuality and progress. You're more ready and willing than ever before to make your own decisions and find your own way in matters. It may be easier than you expected to salvage, or take charge of, or walk away from matters, habits (or people) that aren't good for you.

The more challenging the situation, or other cards in the spread the more work you have ahead of you to discover who you are and what you want. Once you can distinguish the significant from the insignificant and separate fact from fantasy you'll feel more appreciative of your individuality and your purpose in life. Prayer, meditation or even physical exercise could assist you in beginning your positive transformation more easily.

Romantically: The more reassuring the situation, or other cards in the spread, the easier it will be to leave the past in the past and make a fresh start whether by yourself or as a couple, or even with someone new. **The less reassuring the situation,** or other cards in the spread, the more likely it is that you've been wandering in emotional circles for some time. Speaking with a close friend, religious advisor or professional counselor could prevent you from repeating your past mistakes.

At Your Best: you are your own person and happy to be so. **However, should you be overstressed,** or the Eight of Cups appears in reverse, (upside down) you can give

**Card 48
the Eight of Cups**

**Subject Card Eight
stands for future
renovation.**

Keywords:
Emotional/
Renovation

For New Students:
Like the 8th House in
Astrology, our 8's can
often provide clues
concerning the stabil-
ity of our future, with
anyone or anything
that is important to us.

yourself an extraordinarily difficult time in life. Working
with the truth in matters may prove more challenging than
you expected. Any spiritual, social or emotional isolation
you may be laboring under is largely self-imposed.

With Card 48, events tend to promote awareness that,
on some level, you have not been making the most of
yourself.

The Nine of Cups

Events at work and/or at home can give you the feeling that it could be easier than you expected to get into or out of something. However, this is the "wish" card and because it tends to set Karmic wheels in motion, you'd be especially wise to be careful what you wish for now. Although your hopes may be higher than they've been for a while, no matter how strongly you desire something (or someone) now, facing the truth or handling the consequences should your wish come true, may prove more challenging than you expect, or are prepared to handle.

The more encouraging the situation, or other cards in the spread, the easier it will be to get your own way with less effort or resistance than you expected. You could obtain a better deal, better job, or bigger promotion.

The more challenging the situation, or other cards in the spread the more challenging it may be to uphold your ethics in light of temptation. Something may turn out to be a great deal less than you expected. Self-indulgence can be your worst enemy whether you're overestimating other people, matters or yourself!

Romantically: The more reassuring the situation, or other cards in the spread, the easier it may be to obtain a date with, or impress, someone that interests you. **The less reassuring the situation**, or other cards in the spread, the harder it may be to resist the temptation to stray or take unethical advantage of an emotional situation. It may be proving harder than you expected to free yourself from a relationship that no longer pleases you.

At your best: your attitude will be positive and generally optimistic. Commonsense is your guide, making your wishes easier to obtain, because they are more realistic than idealistic. You're happiest when you're making things happen, and you revel in the tangible benefits that

Card 49

the Nine of Cups

Subject Card Nine represents your understanding.

Keywords:

Emotional Understanding

For New Students:
Like the 9th House in Astrology, our 9's can also make it easier or more challenging to expand our outlook while maintaining our beliefs and self-confidence.

accompany your progress. The outcomes that you orchestrate are new starts that could take you farther than you ever dreamed possible. However, should you be overstressed, or the Nine of Cups appears in reverse, (upside down) beware of allowing your ego to overwhelm your commonsense. Your wish may be delayed or prove not to be all that you expect.

With Card 49, the more strongly you desire something (or someone) the more likely you are to obtain your goal whether through genuine effort, or manipulation.

The Ten of Cups

Events at work, home (or both) will heighten your feelings about, memories of, or longing for, togetherness. However, with the Ten of Cups your life can only become what you *make* it – not as you imagine it to be. The less restricted you feel by any one person or matter the more good you can accomplish for all.

The more encouraging the situation, or other cards in the spread, the easier it will be for you and other people to compromise – possibly for the sake of a larger issue. You may take the first step towards healing an emotional breach. This can bring all sorts of good news and good times together. You can make even the most tedious task more enjoyable. It may be almost impossible to determine where your friends begin and family ends.

 The more challenging the situation, or the other cards in the spread the more complex or hopeless matters may feel to be. This can signal emotional disharmony or loss. People who should be closest to you may seem to be deliberately pitting themselves against you and your mutual endeavors. Speaking with a close friend, religious advisor or professional counselor could help you adjust your perspective, or prevent you from making matters worse.

Romantically: The more reassuring the situation, or other cards in the spread, the more you stand to gain from positive social interaction. You could meet your future partner or mate. You may become engaged or get married. This can signal a happy pregnancy or birth. **The less reassuring the situation,** or other cards in the spread, the less likely you and your mate or partner will be able to avoid a serious disagreement or separation. There may be news of an unexpected pregnancy.

At your best: You can resolve your differences of opinion constructively, in a manner that helps you and those you care for continue to get ahead – even when you're moving in opposite directions. Everything you do expresses the joy you feel for life.

Card 50
the Ten of Cups

Subject Card Ten represents Achievement.

Keywords:
Emotional/ Achievement

For New Students:

Like the 10th House in Astrology, since our 10's can also lead us to feel as if we're closer to too, or farther away from achieving our goals, they can also make whatever we're doing more or less enjoyable

However, should you be overstressed, or the Ten of Cups appears in reverse, (upside down) you may be in for a rude awakening. Your "need to be needed" or an inability to resist some form of temptation may prove to be your Achilles heel and possibly lead to your undoing.

Card 50 can inspire you to become more creative and communicative, able to radiate humor, and commonsense. Best of all, should any matters be eluding your control, Card 50 can also inspire you to become more independent and resourceful.

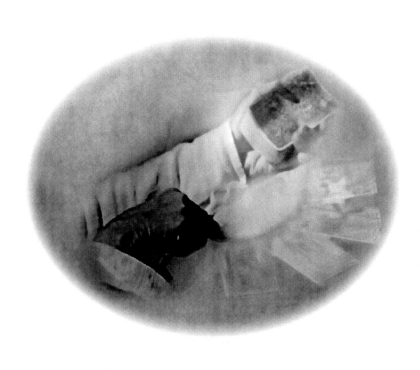

ABOUT SWORDS[1]

Keyword: Challenge

Element: Air

Corresponding Astrological Signs: Aquarius ♒, Gemini ♊, and Libra ♎.

Corresponding Playing Card: Spades

Function: Swords engage your intellect and test your resolve in matters as well as yourself.

---

[1] aka. Daggers, Knives, Leaves, Quills, etc. in some Tarot Decks.

CHAPTER 5

In Tarot, the element of Air corresponds to the suit of Swords, as well as the Astrological Signs, Libra ♎, Aquarius ♒ and Gemini ♊. Air Signs are the most versatile and diverse Signs in the Zodiac, because Air is the most versatile and diverse of all the elements. Like Air Signs, Swords also exemplify your communications and ideas, which correlates to putting thoughts into words and ideas into action, whether to start matters moving or keep them in motion to bring order into chaos or blast everything out of existence–by way of delays or emergencies that suddenly change your plans. Yet thanks to their diversity, by utilizing some additional self-control Swords can also enable you to transform whatever challenges or delays you initiate or encounter into an opportunity to succeed, by lending you a more intellectual and objective approach to handling matters. However, under more stressful conditions, you can become too quick to take offense where none was intended. When reading the RWS deck, the Swords whose illustrations features the Swords in an upright position signify a situation in which you may be able to think more clearly or maintain a positive mindset more easily, thereby enabling your communications to flow more smoothly – if not happily. However, when reading cards that feature the Swords pointing sideways there is a greater possibility of miscommunication – usually due to mixed signals, while the illustrations that feature the Swords pointing downwards signal additional complications that can make matters more challenging. Swords often imply tension that may lead you to behave too offensively or defensively, especially if you consider the issue to be one of principle. The more encouraging the situation or other cards in the spread, you'll meet matters head-on displaying courage and determination that may even surprise you! Your sense of justice, principle and integrity can bring order into chaos. The more challenging the situation or other cards in the spread the more you will need to apply and rely on self-control to turn the tide of events in your favor. Lest you become too self-righteous, you'd be wise to consider whether you are moving in the best, or simply the most convenient direction. Should the majority of your spread consist of Swords, your greatest chal- lenge will be to remain focused upon your ultimate goal. Swords can imply as much — if not more, distraction as inspiration.

KEY POINTS WHEN READING SWORDS

All Swords correlate to the Astrological Air Signs, Gem- ini, Libra and Aquarius.

"Challenging" implies either a busier or more active time period, or situation, whose resolution will require a little more time, patience and thought.

Swords engage your intellect and test your resolve in matters as well as yourself and self-control is the key that can transform any challenges or delays that you initiate or encounter into an opportunity to succeed.

Although Swords can lend you a more intellectual and objective approach to handling matters, under more stressful condi- tions, you can become too quick to take offense where none was intended.

Swords can imply as much –

if not more, distraction as inspiration.

Subject Cards 2-10 often signify situations, advantages, opportunities, moods or obstacles that come out of nowhere, and sometimes pass just as quickly.

THE SWORDS

The King of Swords

Since you are likely to be more outspoken now, it may be easier than usual for you to relate to other people who are the same way. Whatever the situation, the King of Swords can enable you to deal more comfortably with the facts in matters. People from all walks of life, can respect your ability to relate to them - on their level.

The more encouraging the situation, or other cards in the spread, the better prepared you will be to tackle each task or dilemma you encounter. At work and at home, you exude capability and readiness, moving from one matter to the next like a general executing a well-planned campaign. You'll even be less likely to cancel, any legal, medical or dental appointments that may be on your agenda. Although cordial, your manner is as determined as your behavior. Your direct manner can serve you well in meetings or interviews with authority figures.

The more challenging the situation, or other cards in the spread the more likely you are to blame other people for your lack of focus and preparation. Meetings or interviews with authority figures are likely to prove counterproductive. Should you be inclined to take too many matters personally or the wrong way, refusing to discuss matters with an open mind will only compound any misunderstanding that arise.

Romantically: Should your spread contain a hint of romance, your determination to win the object of your affection could be handicapped by your reluctance to make the first move. The more reassuring the situation, or other cards in the spread, the more likely the attraction will be mutual, but not necessarily long-lived. The less reassuring the situation, or other cards in the spread the more challenging and intense your relationship will be because of the "mixed signals" you both employ.

At your best: you can prove to be uncommonly resourceful and self-assertive should your path become blocked by unnecessary protocol or narrow-minded thinking and attitudes.

Card 51
The King of Swords

Kings trigger
or enhance your
initiative.

Keywords:

Challenging/
Initiative

For New Students:
Whatever your gen-
der or situation, the
King can enable you
to set new wheels in
motion or handle on-
going situations more
effectively–whether to
gain an upper hand or
mount a solid defense.

However, should you be overstressed, or the King of Swords appears in reverse, (upside down) you may soon discover that you've placed your trust in the wrong person, or people. The more anxious you are to gain the support or approval of other people, the more likely you are to mishandle matters and create the opposite effect.

With Card 51, even people with whom you seldom agree are likely to be more receptive to your advice, suggestions and opinions at this time.

The Queen of Swords

Here is the warrior Queen! Your awareness and intuitive abilities have a keener edge that can help you avert disaster or calamity at the last possible moment. Whatever your situation, you are as acquisitive as you are inquisitive – seeking to expand your knowledge and horizons – yet cautious about accepting any opportunity, without examining it more closely.

The more encouraging the situation, or other cards in the spread, the more awe-inspiring as well as positive your example will be. At work and at home, you're the epitome of "If I can do it – anyone can" setting an example that's as inspirational as it is effective. Whatever cause or idea you choose to promote or defend is certain to showcase your capabilities. Medically, legally or both, now may be the time to clarify or fine-tune your interests or obligations. Safeguarding your energy and taking better care of your physical health should be first – not last on your list.

The more challenging the situation, or other cards in the spread the more challenging the matters at hand will be. You must beware of putting more wheels in motion than you can control easily. You may have to "pay the piper" now for some type of rash past behavior. At work, home or both, you may soon discover that someone has been playing a dual role of friend and foe in one of your personal or professional relationships.

Romantically: Should your spread contain a hint of romance, your determination to win the object of your affection could cause you to misrepresent yourself. **The more reassuring the situation,** or other cards in the spread, the more likely your attraction may be based upon mutual past emotional disappointments. **The less reassuring the situation,** or other cards in the spread the more you may enjoy the challenge of gaining affection more than the realities of the relationship.

At your best: you're an efficient organizer and planner, who can become irritable when your timetable is disrupted. You

Card 52
The Queen of Swords

Queens can enhance your people and coping skills.

Keywords:
Challenging/ Charm

For New Students:
Whatever your gender or situation, the Queen can enable you to keep everyone and everything, "on the same page," more easily by managing people and cultivating matters with greater efficiency.

REINA DE ESPADAS   REGINA DI SPADE
KÖNIGIN DER SCHWERTER   REINE D'ÉPÉES

QUEEN OF SWORDS

are a shrewd and accurate judge of your emotional and material concerns – always ready and able to negotiate or bargain your way to the top in any endeavor. **However, should you be overstressed** or the Queen of Swords appears in reverse, (upside down) time after time, you can push people and matters too far. One day you're a tyrant, the next you're a martyr. You may soon have to account for a matter you've mishandled.

Card 52 lends you the energy and readiness to make war or promote peace within yourselves, as well as with other people. Whatever your gender, or situation, your people and coping skills are about to be tested or required.

The Knight of Swords

You'd be wise to choose your battles carefully. All Knights are reactionaries. Each Knight has the potential to stimulate a different type of personal behavior. The Knight of Swords can enhance your determination – enabling you to devise a multitude of winning strategies that are as unique as they are resourceful. Yet, no matter how flawless your strategy, you could still lose – unless your goal is more purposeful than pointless. The sooner you recognize what is worth fighting for, the sooner you can put your energy to work for you, rather than against you.

The more encouraging the situation, or other cards in the spread, the greater your courage and the stronger your determination to succeed. At work and at home, it may appear as if you're everywhere at once whenever you're needed. Your "can-do" energy will enable you to accomplish even more matters than you needed to. You'll appear to be as invincible as you feel – taking the helm in matter after matter whether to save the day or start the ball rolling!

The more challenging the situation, or other cards in the spread the harder it will be to summon the energy and focus that you need to keep pace with matters at home and at work. The closer you come to an agreement, the harder it is to finalize matters. Health, dental, or legal emergencies could come out of nowhere. Disagreements could become too intense or ugly. Court dates may be delayed or changed without warning – or notice. Try to be more careful when traveling too; a ticket or a fender-bender could come out of nowhere.

Romantically: Should your spread contain a hint of romance, **the more reassuring the situation,** or other cards in the spread, the stronger, but not necessarily in synch your attraction for one another will be. You may surprise yourself by suddenly becoming engaged, moving in together or getting married. **The less reassuring the situation,** or other cards in the spread the more you will feel as if you're beating your head against a brick wall, whether you're trying to begin or end a relationship. Disagreements could become ugly.

At your best: your skillful manner and resourceful nature can make you appear to be both fearless and inexhaustible.

Card 53
The Knight of Swords

Knights indicate unexpected developments in matters or your behavior.

Keywords:

Challenging/ Adventure

For New Students:

Since Knights tend to produce a "domino" effect, whether it's more expedient to move forward or step back for now, any changes that you make or encounter in one matter, may require making a change in another.

CABALLO DE ESPADAS   CAVALIERE DI SPADE
RITTER DER SCHWERTER   CHEVALIER D'ÉPÉES

KNIGHT OF SWORDS

A team player, your positive belief system is as contagious as it is inspirational – making you a powerful asset as well as a for- midable adversary. However, should you be overstressed, or the Knight of Swords appears in reverse, (upside down) even when you're in the best mood – one wrong word could spoil your day. Should you become more frenzied than flexible, you may soon have to admit you've been wasting more time, energy, emotion or money than you should have.

With Card 53 you can either continue beating your head against brick walls, or temper your determination with diplomacy and move farther ahead in matters at a smoother pace.

The Page of Swords

"No matter how good any news that you receive may be, don't assume that your success is "in the bag." No matter how problematical any news that you receive may be, don't assume that all is lost". With the Page of Swords, you're sure to arrive sooner or later than you expected when traveling. You'd also be wise to beware of small accidents – especially on your own two feet. Pages' sometimes provide a message concerning pregnancy, children or grandchildren under the age of twenty-five. As a rule, with the Page of Swords, the more reassuring the surrounding cards the more surprising – yet welcome the change or news. Whatever transpires may signal a welcome burst of maturity or academic prowess. The less reassuring the surrounding cards the sooner a matter relating to the young person's health, family life, or their social development and personal behavior will become a source of greater interest, concern or both.

Children aside, the more encouraging the situation, or other cards in the spread, the easier you can resolve smaller frustrations and disagreements without blowing matters out of proportion. At work and at home matters as well as your energy level will be a little more erratic and unpredictable.

The more challenging the situation, or other cards in the spread the more likely you are to make a mountain out of a molehill. A small medical or dental problem could rapidly escalate into a major dilemma. So could a small financial oversight, legal matter or misunderstanding. At work, home or both, you may soon have to deal with a disagreement that could take you by surprise.

Romantically: Should your spread contain a hint of romance, the possibility of meeting someone new or becoming closer to, or further estranged from your current mate or partner is likely to stem from how each of you speak to one another in the near future. **The more reassuring the situation,** or other cards in the spread, the more likely you are to experience a "meeting of the minds" or an "aha" moment of understanding and clarification. Witty, even quirky, or profound comments could be the catalyst that brings you closer together with other people. **The less reassuring the situation,** or other cards in the spread, the more likely you are

Card 54
The Page of Swords

Pages signal small matters with the potential to grow larger – a work in progress.

Keywords:
Challenging/ Surprises

For New Students:

Aside from pregnancy, children and grandchildren, the Page can also signal the figurative "birth" of new ideas and opportunities – or simply a larger number of small inconveniences.

SOTA DE ESPADAS   FANTE DI SPADE
BUBE DER SCHWERTER   VALET D'ÉPÉES

PAGE OF SWORDS

to notice a slightly less appealing side of each others character or personality that could serve as an early warning or the final straw.

At Your Best: you'll instinctively know how to make "the element of surprise" work for you. You can appear to feel "at home" in virtually any social climate. **However, should you be overstressed** or the Page of Swords appears in reverse, (upside down) your child-like charm, contagious enthusiasm, and overall appeal, can mask a very conniving, cunning and callous nature.

With Card 54, you'll get farther ahead in the long run and come closer to maintaining your present agenda by setting small goals that are easier to accomplish.

The Ace of Swords

The Ace of Swords represents a possibility of winning or losing more than you expect. **The more encouraging the situation,** or other cards in the spread, the more likely you are to emerge as the victor in matters at work or at home. Whatever the reason, you're ready to be more self-assertive. Whether or not everyone likes you, they'll have to respect your fortitude and they're sure to understand where you're coming from. This could bring news of a promotion at work, some type of legal or medical victory, or success in achieving a professional or publishing contract.

The more challenging the situation, or other cards in the spread the more likely you are to encounter an unexpected legal, medical or dental emergency – or job crisis whether for you or someone close to you.

Romantically: It's not unusual for the Ace of Swords to represent a relationship or attraction where one or both of the parties are waiting for the other to make a choice, decision or the first move. Should your spread contain a hint of romance, whether or not you are romantically involved, this is a time when you more easily identify and come to terms with any "missing factors" in your social or romantic life. **The more reassuring the situation,** or other cards in the spread, the less hesitant you will be to take the first step, whether to clear the air or let someone know that you care. **The less reassuring the situation,** or other cards in the spread, the more likely some type of emotional misrepresentation or misinterpretation may be revealed. Discovering where each of you stand in the others estimation, will make it easier to confront the future, come what may.

At your best: you're very conscious of your ability to make or break matters, as well as the people who are counting on you. At this time you may become more intuitive in the company of other people.

However, should you be overstressed, or the Ace of Swords appears in reverse, (upside down) whether due to matters beyond your control, or poor judgment, you are likely to

Card 55
The Ace of Swords

Aces signify an inevitable showdown.

Keywords:

Challenging/ Crisis or Reward

For New Students:

The Ace indicates an approaching break, or breakthrough in matters. The better prepared you are, the sooner you'll begin making the most of your new situation.

AS DE ESPADAS
AS DER SCHWERTER   1   ASSO DI SPADE
AS D'ÉPÉES

ACE OF SWORDS

encounter an unexpected delay, frustration or other emergency. In some instances, an unhealthy mix of ego, temper and misguided principle, could undermine matters for you. In other instances you may be too easily distracted and simply waste more time and energy than you can afford.

With Card 55, there's likely to be a little more controversy or adversity swirling around someone you know – or the reasoning behind something you've said, or done! Yet, even upsets, will be accompanied by a moment of crystal clarity when you realize you are "better off" or better equipped to handle matters than you expected.

The Two of Swords
Depending upon the situation, personal determination can be your perfect companion or worst enemy. There is some uncertainty about a matter at work, at home, or both. You may be waiting for an answer, formulating a reply or preparing to initiate a request or discussion. Despite your desire to be "brave" or "do the right thing" in matters, you're only human. Whatever your situation, the Two of Swords can enable you to develop a more reliable method to help you cope – whether with situations you can't change, losses you can't prevent or people that you can't seem to please.

The more encouraging the situation, or other cards in the spread, the easier you can play the "waiting-game" in matters now. Any delays you encounter now are more likely to work in your favor strengthening your position as well as your resolve. Whether personally, medically or legally, allowing yourself to take one day, one dream, and one step at a time now can help you get back on course while meditation can help you relax and retain your focus.

The more challenging the situation, or other cards in the spread the more challenging it will be for you to remain impartial and patient. Allowing impatience and frustration to control your behavior, or dictate your attitude, could cause you to say and do things that will undermine the cause you are hoping to save, salvage or promote. Whether in the interest of self-preservation or self-advancement, you may be the instigator or cause of quarrels between other people.

At your best: the more in tune you are with yourself, despite any conflict that may be swirling around you, the easier you can retain your own peace of mind or resolve matters to everyone's best interest and satisfaction – including your

Card 56
The Two of Swords

Subject Card Two signifies your attachments.

Keywords:

Challenging/ Attachments

For New Students:
Like the 2nd House in Astrology, despite its fondness for company, our 2's also trigger an awareness of how much we're receiving in return from other people and matters.

own. **However, should you be overstressed,** or the Two of Swords appears in reverse, (upside down) irrational fears and anxieties may arise when you least expect them.

With Card 56, whether you're overconfident, in doubt, or under pressure it can be very tempting to either do nothing, or follow the course of least-resistance – knowing full well that you'll regret it later.

The Three of Swords

On one or more levels, this is a card that can enable you to come to better terms with yourself, readjust your focus, or maybe both! A matter at work, at home, or both, could pose a challenge to your rationality as well as your agenda. The Three of Swords is often associated with terms such as treachery, sorrow and deceit, which paint a most unpleasant picture. Whatever your situation, the Three of Swords signals a breakdown in communications or negotiations that should also trigger a personal wake-up-call.

The more encouraging the situation, or other cards in the spread, the less surprised you will be by a piece of bad news that you may hear or matters that don't go your way. You may be more relieved that a matter is finally resolved and ready to proceed with an alternative plan of action. In some instances, by summoning additional patience and extending a little more understanding you may even re-establish communication or prevent a matter from becoming worse.

The more challenging the situation, or other cards in the spread the greater your surprise or disappointment will be with a particular outcome, event or person. The more challenging it is to cope with matters, the more important it is not to forsake your faith and hope. Emotional upsets, last-minute cancellations, or a small series of minor misunderstandings at work and home can leave you feeling especially uncooperative, or confused and over sensitive. Talking with a close friend, religious advisor or professional counselor could help.

At your best: you're a deep-thinker who tries to consider every genuine and potential aspect of matters before you make a decision or promise. Even when it takes a little longer before you can laugh at some of your mistakes, you never fail to learn from them.

Card 57
The Three of Swords

Subject Card Three is for thinking and networking.

Keywords:

Challenging/ Thinking & Networking

For New Students:

Like the 3rd House in Astrology, our 3's also signal news, ideas and activity that can keep us in-touch and on our toes, or lead us to change our mind at the last minute.

However, should you be overstressed, or the Three of Swords self-sabotage, or self-pity appears in reverse (upside down) can be your greatest enemy. Misappropriation of your time, talent and energy can cause you to repeatedly devise schemes and short-cuts that lead to nowhere.

Although Card 57 does signal an upcoming delay, disappointment or loss – more often than not, at least part of our disappointment stems from a matter, person or even one of our own talents that we either overestimated or underestimated.

The Four of Swords

The Four of Swords is all about trying to decide what your next move should be. Depending upon your situation you may feel as if you're in limbo, or on top of the world! A matter or event at work, at home, or both, may shortly rejuvenate and restore, or jeopardize your security and motivation. Whatever your situation, you've recently ended or are in the process of concluding a chapter in your life and trying to decide what your next move should be. Whether professionally, medically or emotionally, recouping your energy and regrouping your initiative is a necessary part of this process. Whether you're feeling more or less confident about matters now you'd be wise to avoid any temptation to take matters to extremes, either by trying to do too much, or too little.

The more encouraging the situation, or other cards in the spread, the more likely it is that you have reached a plateau in life. The more content you are with your location, the more energetically and resourcefully you will work to secure your position, making it easier to resist outside distractions and temptations that might disrupt your comfort zone, The happier you are with your employment, social life or relationships the longer and easier you can maintain your status quo by not jumping to conclusions, making mountains out of molehills or being to quick to assume the worst before you know all the facts in matters.

The more challenging the situation, or other cards in the spread the more likely it is that too many matters are hanging in limbo. Whether you're trying to wish a problem away, or believe that you can still save or resurrect a dead issue, denying the facts will do more harm than good. Talking with a close friend, religious advisor or professional counselor could help.

At your best: whether you feel as if you're running in first or last place now, you know that accomplishing your dreams and goals is never out of the question. At work and home,

Card 58
The Four of Swords

Subject Card Four is all about your sense of belonging and security.

Keywords:

Challenging/ Belonging and Security

For New Students:
Like the 4th House in Astrology, our 4's signal an increase or decrease in our material and domestic activities, that can strengthen or disturb our sense of belonging and security.

you approach matters with kindness, tempered by wisdom. **However, should you be overstressed,** or the Four of Swords appears in reverse, (upside down) although your options are likely to be more limited than limitless, whenever you're right, you'll demand apologies and detailed explanations, but when you're wrong, you won't care to discuss matters. Refusing to confront one issue in a timely manner will only complicate, if not jeopardize other matters.

With Card 58 matters simply are or are not happening in your life.

The Five of Swords

Beware of overstepping your boundaries now in matters, at home, at work or both. Frustration with matters at home, at work, or both, could incite you to take steps you should have taken before. Impatience or over-confidence in matters could incite you to take unnecessary or foolish risks. Whether or not your thought process accelerates, since you're likely to feel more restless, tense or edgy, – without even realizing it you could make at least one mountain out of a molehill now.

The more encouraging the situation, or other cards in the spread, the easier you can toss aside reluctance or self-doubt to address or proceed with matters you've been wondering or worrying about. Whether or not you're happy with the response, you'll be glad you've brought matters out in the open and wonder why you waited so long. You may begin to exhibit an uncanny ability to calculate the odds more accurately now, making it easier to identify and eliminate potential problems without becoming distracted. The stronger your determination to succeed the more quickly and easily you can apply new methods and tactics that make your task easier.

The more challenging the situation, or other cards in the spread the more you need to beware of overstepping your bounds in matters. Whether you've been taking too many matters, people, yourself or your health for granted, you could receive a comeuppance or a response that rocks your world or wounds your pride. Respect your intuition and beware taking unnecessary risks with your physical safety. Medically, you or someone close to you may be more susceptible to unexpected side effects from medication, or it may prove more challenging for medical authorities to accurately diagnose or treat an ailment.

At your best: since your determination to do the right thing, fuels your refusal to take "no" for an answer from yourself, it can pave your way to success. If necessary, you may even push aside your fear for yourself and concern for your comfort to help other people. You may even find it easier to identify the source of your dissatisfaction and come to terms with it now.

Card 59
The Five of Swords

Subject Card Five is a card of conflict and speculation.

Keywords:

Challenging/ Conflict & Speculation

For New Students:

Like the 5th House in Astrology, our 5's can also trigger an unexpected conflict of interest between our logic and emotions, in matters ranging from duty, to friendship, finance, romance - or parenting.

However, should you be overstressed, or the Five of Swords appears in reverse, (upside down) you can be too easily distracted or annoyed, which could lead to any number of misunderstandings, or even an unfortunate accident.

With Card 59, you can be just as much of an enigma to yourself as a challenge to other people. This is the ultimate "do-it-yourself" card, and like it or not, it can enhance your self-reliance.

The Six of Swords

Whether personally, professionally, legally or medically you've been going in circles and need to unwind. Whatever your situation "here we go again" is the key phrase and battle cry for you and the Six of Swords. Your desire to reach a new destination, or achieve a better understanding of yourself, matters or people will require patience and courage. If travel is on your agenda, you may choose to revisit someplace from your past. If travel is not on your agenda, you may have to take an unexpected journey. As long as the quest you choose to pursue broadens rather than narrows your horizons and perspective you can't help but win – though perhaps not in the manner or time frame you expected to.

The more encouraging the situation, or other cards in the spread, the easier you can extricate yourself from pointless situations or harmful habits that limit your personal progress and interfere with your ability to honor worthwhile commitments. Someone that you enjoy may unexpectedly reappear in your life.

The more challenging the situation, or other cards in the spread the more likely your true strength of character will be tested. Someone or something may disappoint you – yet again. People, matters, medical or legal issues that you thought were resolved may make an unexpected and unwelcome reappearance. The more vulnerable you are to distractions (especially but not exclusively) from the wrong influences or people, the more likely you'll find yourselves having to start over in matters from finance to health to romance.

At your best: you are patient, steadfast, resilient conscientious and somewhat cynical. Your preference for handling matters yourself is as inspirational as the resourceful methods with which you can achieve your goals. **However, should you be overstressed,** or the Six of Swords appears in reverse, (upside down) you may be wasting too much time, energy and effort believing too strongly in matters and people that are wrong

Card 60
The Six of Swords

Subject Card Six represents commitment.

Keywords:

Challenging/ Commitments

For New Students:

Like the 6th House in Astrology, our 6's can also signal situations that can enhance or disrupt our peace of mind, as we strive to keep pace with matters and people that comprise our daily routine.

for you, and not believing enough in yourself. The harder you cling to self-defeating habits, thinking or (espe- cially) emotional patterns the more likely you are to repeat the same mistakes.

With Card 60, whether you need to stop making excuses, or stop accepting them, now is the time to find a better way to handle yourself and matters.

The Seven of Swords

Events may put you and other people "on the spot" concerning your integrity or the quality of your relationship. Whether you are feeling overconfident, or under-confident don't be too quick to believe everything you hear and watch what you say. Although the Seven of Swords can imply outright thievery of an object, or from a source you didn't expect – more often than not, it's a warning against stealing from yourself by wasting your time, effort, talents and emotion on non-productive relationships or endeavors.

The more encouraging the situation, or other cards in the spread, the easier it will be for you to diplomatically extricate yourself from becoming too involved with matters that don't concern you. Much to your surprise, someone may be less likely to lie to you and more likely to keep a promise or appointment with you. You may be more flirtatious. An opportunity for you to play matchmaker (or be matched up with someone else) could turn out better than you expect. You may realize, a little sooner than later that you have not fallen as far behind in matters or lost as much as you feared.

The more challenging the situation, or other cards in the spread the more careful you should be of your possessions, health and safety. Don't be too quick to believe everything you hear, and watch what you say. Something you've said or done could return to haunt you. You may be deceived or a deception that you planned could backfire. The greater the temptation to tell a "white" lie or embellish the truth the more you should resist doing so. The more dependent you have become upon other people's affection or opinions the easier that dependence can sap your strength, erode your individuality, and prevent you from effectively standing up for yourself.

Card 61
the Seven of
Swords

Subject Card Seven corresponds to your relationships.

Keywords:
Challenging / Relationships

For New Students:
Like the 7ᵗʰ House in Astrology, our 7's can also signal an unexpected turn of events – for better or worse, concerning our relationships, at work,home or both.

ESPADAS
SCHWERTER
7
SPADE
ÉPÉES

SWORDS

At your best: a positive attitude and patience can lend you the additional wisdom and patience to meet and beat your problems and detractors. **However, should you be over-stressed,** or the Seven of Swords appears in reverse, (upside down) matters can feel more hopeless than they really are.

With Card 61, the more you care for or dislike someone, the easier those feelings could undermine your objectivity – if you allow them too.

The Eight of Swords

There's some extra work, or news coming your way that could upset your day, preempt your agenda, and lead you to feel momentarily, "bound and tied" by circumstances that you can neither prevent or control. Whether your disposition is surly or sweet, you have the panache and savior fare to appear as if you've resolved matters even when you haven't.

The more encouraging the situation, or other cards in the spread, the more likely your frustration will be of a shorter duration. You're greatest irritation is likely to stem from the fact that other people waited so long to notify you or to take action.

The more challenging the situation, or other cards in the spread, whether you or someone close to you has waited too long to attend a health, personal or professional matter, or you never saw the problem coming, getting matters back on track will require a little more time and effort. The good news is that meeting these challenges are more likely to make you stronger in the long run. If believing that it's no use to try and change your thinking and direction has become a habit, you may be viewing the matters that are holding back as "blessings" that give you the strength to shoulder self-imposed burdens. Talking with a friend, or perhaps a professional counselor could help.

At your best: at work and home, you're uncommonly resourceful when it comes to delegating responsibility and tackling obstacles that could threaten your progress or security. You can be counted on to devise a logical solution that can resolve any type of dilemma. **However, should you be overstressed**, or the Eight of Swords appears in reverse, (upside down) you may be a willing prisoner and victim of narrow thinking, strong passions

Card 62
the Eight of Swords

Subject Card Eight stands for future renovation.

Keywords:

Challenging/ Renovation

For New Students:

Like the 8ᵗʰ House in Astrology, our 8's can often provide clues concerning the stability of our future, with anyone or anything that is important to us.

(or both) – more concerned with today instead of tomorrow. Should this be the case you may soon have to work much harder than you think, to prevent matters from overwhelming you.

With Card 62, the longer you wait to confront your inhibitions, or irritation the longer you'll have to settle for just getting by in matters where you could and should have come out ahead.

The Nine of Swords

Although you can clearly envision what you want to do, the more important that something (or someone) else is to you, the more challenging it can be for you to face the facts. Whether you have a strong desire to go into seclusion to escape the confusion in your life, or feel overwhelmed by a burning to desire to be the best or first in everything, or you're allowing other people's opinions, problems (or both) to consume your life, your preoccupation is doing you more harm than good. Making yourself take a break now will enable you to recharge your own energy and refresh your perspective.

The more encouraging the situation, or other cards in the spread, the sooner you are likely to realize that you're making mountains out of molehills, or laboring under a burden of undeserved guilt. No matter what your situation, you really do have more options than your pride, emotions or principles are allowing you to consider.

The more challenging the situation, or other cards in the spread the more challenging it may be to let other people fight their own battles or live their own life, but you must allow them the freedom to do so. The more willing you are to consider other options and points of view the more likely you could reach the road to recovery, a little sooner than later. The less willing you are to consider other alternatives, the longer you will remain a "slave to anxiety." Meditation, yoga, speaking with a religious advisor, close friend or professional counselor could help you.

At your best: you can allow your sense of humor to save the day and your sanity whenever you begin to feel overwhelmed by matters. You can use your experience and

Card 63
the Nine of Swords

Subject Card Nine represents your understanding.

Keywords:

Challenging/
Understanding

For New Students:
Like the 9th House in Astrology, our 9's can make it easier or more of a challenge to expand our outlook while maintaining our beliefs and self-confidence.

ESPADAS
SCHWERTER

9

SPADE
ÉPÉES

SWORDS

compassion to help others help themselves grow through similar trials. **However, should you be overstressed,** or the Nine of Swords appears in reverse, (upside down) obtaining what, or who you want, regardless of the consequences can become an unwise – even unhealthy preoccupation.

With Card 63, allowing yourself to walk away from a situation, or relationship that can't be salvaged just now, can be as challenging as it is essential to your well-being.

The Ten of Swords

Whatever it seems as if everything is happening too quickly or that nothing is moving at all, giving in to the feeling that you are carrying "the weight of the world on your shoulders" is not in your best interests now. This card is just as likely to appear when success is within your grasp as it is to appear when you're grappling with a recent loss or setback. So whatever your situation, just beware a tendency to imagine the worst, or create self- imposed restrictions, such as "I can't".

The more encouraging the situation, or other cards in the spread, the more quickly – if not easily – you'll be able to get matters and your attitude back on track by confronting rather than denying your duties and responsibilities. Taking a second look at matters now, will reveal a few flaws that you weren't willing to recognize before and make it easier to follow a more resourceful course of action that can still enable you to succeed and possibly grow farther than you expected. You'll probably even notice some "light at the end of the tunnel" more quickly than you expected.

The more challenging the situation, or other cards in the spread the harder you may have to work to rejuve- nate or redirect your ambition and sense of purpose. Should clinical depression or another medical condition be compounding your sense of loss, betrayal or deser- tion, now's the time to "pick yourself up, dust yourself off and start all over again". By taking one day and one matter at a time you can begin to re-capture your self-confidence, and stop victimizing yourself. You also won't be so quick to manufacture reasons to feel suspicious or nervous when matters are going well. Meditation, yoga, speaking with a religious advisor, close friend or professional counselor could help.

Card 64
the Ten of Swords

Subject Card Ten is a card for Achievement.

Keywords:

Challenging/ Achievement

For New Students:
Like the 10th House in Astrology, since our 10's can also lead us to feel as if we're closer to, or farther away from achieving our goals, they can also make whatever we're doing, more or less enjoyable.

At your best: you won't give up on yourself and you're always willing to help others who are trying to help themselves. Your ability to combine humor and fact with clever analogies helps you get your point across more effectively. **However, should you be overstressed,** or the Ten of Swords appears in reverse, (upside down) you can be too quick to assume all is lost, and begin burning your bridges, the moment matters don't appear to be going your way.

Although Card 64, can sometimes make it difficult to feel as good as you deserve to, about you and your endeavors giving in to a "what's-the-use" attitude, solves nothing.

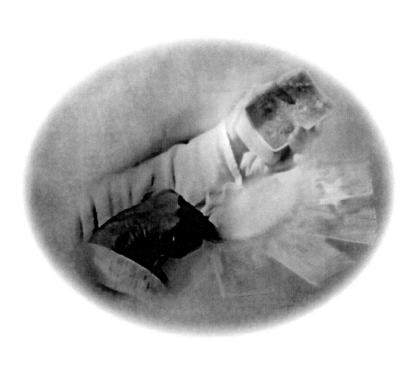

ABOUT PENTACLES[1]

Keyword: Ambition

Element: Earth

Corresponding Astrological Signs: Taurus ♉, Virgo ♍ and Capricorn ♑.

Corresponding Playing Card: Clubs.

Function: Reaping harvest, breaking new ground and planting new seeds in economic and emotional matters.

---

[1] Pentacles* aka. Coins, Disks, Bells, etc. in some Tarot Decks.

175

CHAPTER 6

In the Tarot, the Earth element corresponds to the suit of Pentacles, as well as the Astrological Signs of Capricorn ♑, Taurus ♉ and Virgo ♍. Earth Signs are the most consistent and persistent signs in the zodiac just like the Earth itself. Like the Earth Signs, Pentacles, can imply establishment and continuity or disruption concerning your economic and emotional concerns. They can suggest your best opportunities for material acquisition, stability, advancement and control, as well as provide a warning against or an explanation for a material crisis – factors that also influence personal self-esteem and relation- ships. Pentacles are often associated with finalizing mat- ters or implementing changes that have been planned in advance – but whatever the situation, they encourage a more cautious approach and practical (or down to earth) outlook. Under more stressful conditions, although Pentacles can also represent seemingly immovable obstacles, the more encouraging the situation, whether sooner or later your persistence and effort are sure to be rewarded. The more challenging the situation, the more likely, economy may have to be your watchword – at least temporarily. The harvest you are about to reap in matters may not yield as much as you anticipated, or breaking new ground may prove more challenging than you expected. Should Pentacles comprise the majority of your spread, you can expect to encounter varying degrees of fluctuation in either or both your material and personal (or emotional) concerns.

KEY POINTS WHEN READING PENTACLES

All Pentacles correlate to the Astrological Earth Signs, Taurus ♉, Virgo ♍ and Capricorn ♑.

"Ambitious" refers to your need or desire for economic as well as emotional, acquisition, stability, and advancement.

Since Pentacles can imply establishment and continuity, or disruption concerning your economic and emotional concerns they always encourage you to take a more cautious approach and a more practical (or down to earth) outlook in matters.

Pentacles are synonymous with financial and professional advancement, material acquisition, or material crisis—factors that also influence personal self-esteem and relationships.

Subject Cards 2-10 often signify situations, advantages, opportunities, moods or obstacles that come out of nowhere, and sometimes pass just as quickly.

THE PENTACLES

The King of Pentacles

The King of Pentacles can inspire you to consider new avenues for economic or emotional, advancement and enrichment. It can enhance your sense of humor and dependability, enabling you to put both to work for your material and professional or even emotional advantage.

The more encouraging the situation, or other cards in the spread, the more likely your financial concerns will flow more smoothly. This could be the right time to apply for a loan – or discover that your loan or credit application has been approved. Now could be the time to seek a promotion or a raise in pay. You might even receive one or the other without asking! Matters at work and at home are beginning to shape up; some are even beginning to yield positive return on the effort you've invested. Meetings or interviews with authority figures are likely to go extremely well. You may get along better with members of the opposite sex than you have for some time.

The more challenging the situation, or other cards in the spread, the less generous you and other people will be with one another – at work and at home. You may feel as if everyone you know and everything you're doing is an impediment to your advancement. Since you know this isn't true, try meditating before bedtime. It can help release your inner tension and may reveal the true source of your dissatisfaction.

Romantically: should your spread contain a hint of romance, you'll be more inclined to consider settling down. You'll also be more critical of, and selective about, your romantic choices. You may decide to offer or accept a date, declaration of love, or perhaps a marriage proposal. **The more reassuring the situation,** or other cards in the spread, the more likely it is that you the object of your affection may embrace a similar type of goal or ambition. **The less reassuring the situation,** or other cards in the spread, the more likely you and the object of your affection may be too critical or controlling of one another.

At your best: you exude a quiet sense of dependability that can make you indispensable to even the most independent, as well

Card 65
the King of Pentacles

Kings trigger or enhance your initiative.

Keywords:

Ambitious/ Initiative

For New Students:

Whatever your gender or situation, the King can enable you to set new wheels in motion, or handle ongoing situations more effectively – whether to gain an upper hand in matters or mount a solid defense.

REY DE OROS   RE DI DENARI
KÖNIG DER MÜNZEN   ROI DE DENIERS

KING OF PENTACLES

as important people. **However, should you be overstressed,** or the King of Pentacles appears in reverse, (upside down) you'd be wise to avoid promoting or becoming involved in get-rich-quick schemes, as well as, sudden romantic attractions – both of which are likely to promise more than they will deliver. Should you feel that life is turning against you, it could just be that your past is catching up with you.

Card 65 can test or reward habits and behavior patterns that have become your second nature. For example: spending too much or too little money, time or emotion on matters the harder it is for you to relinquish traits that are doing you more harm than good the longer it will take before you attain the happiness and security you deserve.

The Queen of Pentacles

Whatever the situation, achieving bottom-line results and answers is, (or will be) your main objective. Whether you're waiting to move on, or ahead in life, the Queen of Pentacles can enable you to use your time more productively.

The more encouraging the situation, or other cards in the spread (at work and at home), your patience and clarity will allow you to make fewer mistakes. You're willingness to make personal sacrifices, whether for the benefit of others or a larger matter, sets an ideal example. Your ability to drive a hard, but fair bargain wins other people's respect and lends you additional confidence. Now could be the time to seek, or receive a promotion or a raise in pay. You're more appreciative of quality versus quantity. In larger and smaller ways, you're becoming more self-assertive and independent.

The more challenging the situation or other cards in the spread, you may have to become more self-sufficient or accept more responsibility than you feel you're ready (or care to) to handle. Yoga or meditation will help prevent any unresolved feelings of guilt or a tendency to believe that you're being blamed or treated unfairly from triggering a depression.

Romantically: should your spread contain a hint of romance, you may feel more secure about taking a relationship to the next level or more confident about starting over – whether with someone from your past or someone new. **The more reassuring the situation**, or other cards in the spread, the easier it will be for you and the object of your affection to retain each other's interest. **The less reassuring the situation**, or other cards in the spread, the more likely you or the object of your affection may speak for the other person without consulting them. This could lead to a difference of opinion about control.

At your best: you have a deep loyalty to your goals and apply strict concentration to your methods. Your competent manner gives the impression that you can handle anything and your

Card 66
the Queen of Pentacles

Queens can enhance
your people and
coping skills.

Keywords:

Ambitious/Charm.

For New Students:
Whatever your gender
or situation, the Queen
can enable you to keep
everyone and every-
thing, "on the same
page", more easily by
managing people and
cultivating matters
more efficiently.

REINA DE OROS · REGINA DI DENARI · KÖNIGIN DER MÜNZEN · REINE DE DENIERS

QUEEN OF PENTACLES

positive example inspires others to follow your lead. **However,
should you be overstressed** or the Queen of Pentacles appears
in reverse, (upside down) beware of becoming too sure of
yourself, or too fond of power and material possessions. Med-
dling in others' affairs – under the guise of acting in their best
interests is more likely to work against your best interests.

With Card 66 the happier you are with yourself, the easier you
can relax and take other people and take matters as they come–
with less worry, thereby avoiding the temptation to deny their
existence..

The Knight of Pentacles

Taking a more logical approach to matters now, can move mountains. All Knights are reactionaries. Each Knight has the potential to stimulate a different type of personal behavior. The Knight of Pentacles can enhance your patience for working out the details in matters that pertain to your economic and emotional growth and security.

The more encouraging the situation, or other cards in the spread, the easier you can begin planning ambitious long-range projects such as beginning or expanding your own busi- ness, buying or selling a home, or gathering data to secure a promotion or better job. You're particularly aware of your duties and responsibilities and take great pride in accomplishing everything to the best of your ability.

The more challenging the situation, or other cards in the spread, the more suspicious and critical you'll be of even the best advice or information. Forcing yourself to make decisions because you choose to believe you have no choice will cause you to make choices you'll regret.

Romantically: should your spread contain a hint of romance, you could become involved in a secret love affair or become involved in a group activity that could lead to better romantic opportunities. Socially and romantically, you won't be as interested in pursuing or continuing relationships with people who simply want to "live for and in the moment." **The more reassuring the situation,** or other cards in the spread, the more likely you and the object of your affection will prefer getting together in quiet surroundings, rather than, a rambunctious night on the town. **The less reassuring the situation,** or other cards in the spread, if you're not behaving like a wet blanket you may feel as if your partner is.

Card 67
the Knight of Pentacles

Knights indicate unexpected developments in matters or your behavior.

Keywords:
Ambitious/ Adventure

For New Students:
Since Knights tend to produce a "domino" effect, whether it's more expedient to move forward, or step back for now, any changes that you make in one matter, may require making a change in another.

CABALLO DE OROS   CAVALIERE DI DENARI
RITTER DER MÜNZEN   CHEVALIER DE DENIERS

KNIGHT OF PENTACLES

At your best: personal mediocrity is an unacceptable alternative in your eyes. **However, should you be overstressed,** or the Knight of Pentacles appears in reverse, (upside down) you can become too pessimistic or disinclined to do more than necessary to get someone or something to leave you alone. Any reluctance on your part, to take action in matters before it's too late may result in (or aggravate) ongoing problems at home, at work, or both.

With Card 67 a logical approach can minimize the danger or effects from smaller rockslides of opposition.

The Page of Pentacles

Whatever the situation, you can expect a small opportunity to gain some type of advantage – though it may be something that others might overlook, or consider too much work. Pages sometimes provide a message concerning pregnancy, children or grandchildren under the age of twenty-five. As a rule, with the Page of Pentacles, the more supportive the surrounding cards the more likely matters are falling into place just as you had planned or hoped and maybe both. This is a good time to consider whether or not to have a child (or another child) because you're better equipped to determine the advantages and disadvantages. The less supportive the surrounding cards the sooner a matter relating to the young persons health, family life, or their social development and personal behavior may become a source of greater interest, concern or both. This is not a good time to consider whether or not to have a child because whatever you decide is likely to be for the wrong reasons.

Children aside, the more encouraging the situation, or other cards in the spread, the stronger your attraction to people and matters that are more sensible than sensational. Even the shortest business trip has the potential to introduce new contacts that could enrich your professional future. You may become more interested in pursuing hobbies and entertainments that serve a more practical than idealistic purpose. You may even pursue the possibility of turning a hobby into a full-time job.

The more challenging the situation, or other cards in the spread, the more challenging it will be for you to gain even a slight advantage or break in matters at work and at home. You could make small financial or emotional miscalculations that rapidly snowball into a major inconvenience or disagreement.

Romantically: Should your spread contain a hint of romance, this time period could mark a significant turning point in your emotional and social development. **The more reassuring the situation,** or other cards in the spread, becoming involved – or more involved in events sponsored by your community, workplace or place of worship could hold the key towards a more rewarding social life. Should you have a current date mate or partner, now may be the time to begin planning a more permanent future together. **The less reassuring the situation,** or other

Card 68
the Page of Pentacles

Pages signal small matters with the potential to grow larger – a work in progress.

Keywords:

Ambitious/Surprises

For New Students:

Aside from pregnancy, children and grandchildren, the Page can also signal the figurative "birth" of new ideas and opportunities – or simply a larger number of small inconveniences.

PAGE OF PENTACLES

cards in the spread, the easier and more quickly your (or your partners) head could be turned by other people that appear to promise more than they intend to deliver.

At your best: the more willing you are to compromise with matters and other people now, the more you stand to gain in the long-run. At home, work or both, even the smallest opportunities can lead to future gain or advantage. **However, should you be overstressed,** or the Page of Pentacles appears in reverse, (upside down) a series of smaller miscalculations could rapidly snowball into a major inconvenience or disagreement. You may become irrationally obsessive, paranoid and secretive.

With Card 68, the stronger your self-confidence the more quickly you can master and apply new ideas, that could fortify your current position, expand your horizons – or both. The stronger your self doubts the greater your gullibility.

The Ace of Pentacles

An opportunity could literally "fall into your lap", or a dilemma could prove to be a "blessing in disguise" – possibly even one of each! **The more encouraging the situation,** or other cards in the spread, the more likely some type of opportunity will literally fall into your lap. Purchasing or selling property, job promotions, better job offers, residence changes, redecorating your home, inheritances, legal settlements and "lucky wins" all fall under the jurisdiction of the Ace of Pentacles. Someone may repay a small amount of money they borrowed from you. You may be relieved of a financial obligation.

The more challenging the situation, or other cards in the spread, the more likely you are to encounter an unexpected and unwelcome financial burden or delay. Repairs as well as ordinary expenditures may prove more costly than you anticipated, or you may become so preoccupied with one person or matter that you begin to ignore everything else.

Romantically: Finance is often interwoven with the Ace of Pentacles. Should your spread contain a hint of romance, the opportunity to meet someone new may come your way in any number of mundane ways, such as a change in your employment (or work schedule) to making a simple purchase – or costly repair. Established couples may begin making plans for a new child, home, vehicle, dream vacation or second honeymoon.

The more reassuring the situation, or other cards in the spread, the better your chances to obtain retain or recapture material and emotional stability. **The less reassuring the situation,** or other cards in the spread, personal spending habits or excessive professional obligations may each play a role in complicating or dismantling long-term relationships, as well as short-term attractions.

Card 69
the Ace of Pentacles

Aces signify an
inevitable showdown.

Keywords:

**Ambitious/
Crisis or Reward**

For New Students:
The Ace indicates an
approaching break or
breakthrough in matters.
The better prepared you
are, the sooner you'll
begin making the most
of your new situation.

At your best: you can be relied on to minimize the danger
from others' mistakes, carelessness inexperience or egotis-
tical blundering. **However, should you be overstressed,**
or the Ace of Pentacles appears in reverse, (upside down)
the more likely you are to encounter an unexpected financial expense, or delay and the more manipulative you can
become.

With Card 69, no you can experience a great deal of Spiritual enrichment. Even upsets will be accompanied by a
moment of crystal clarity, when you realize you are "better off," or better equipped to handle matters than you
expected.

The Two of Pentacles

Multi-tasking can (or may need to) be your specialty now. In addition to balancing our budget and schedule, with the Two of Pentacles, it's not unusual for romantic, financial or even legal opportunities, as well as a stroke of unexpected good fortune to crop up when and where you least expect it.

The more encouraging the situation, or other cards in the spread, the easier it will be for you to juggle matters on your agenda. This is a good time to review and possibly restructure your economic future – focusing on long-range benefits. It's easier for you to separate the essential from the non-essential issues in your life and recognize your priorities. Your per- sistence, only accentuates your irresistibility. Multi-tasking can enable each project you complete to flow effortlessly into the next – allowing you to accomplish more to your satisfaction, in less time than usual. At work and home, any matters that begin moving at a slower pace can give you time to catch your breath and catch up with other projects.

The more challenging the situation, or other cards in the spread, the more susceptible you'll be to citing a real or imaginary illness as a means of avoiding matters and people that you don't want to face. Financially, you may need to "rob Peter to pay Paul" for a little while. If matters aren't going as you intended or hoped, try to remember that fate isn't trying to punish you, but nudge you in a better direction.

At your best: You can talk anyone into giving you a bargain, a break or another chance.

However, should you be overstressed or the Two of Pentacles appears in reverse, (upside down) unrealistic thinking

Card 70
the Two of Pentacles

Subject Card Two signifies your attachments.

Keywords:

Ambitious/ Attachments

For New Students:

Like the 2ⁿᵈ House in Astrology, despite its fondness for company, our 2's trigger an awareness of how much we're receiving in return from other people and matters.

OROS
MÜNZEN

2

DENARI
DENIERS

PENTACLES

may result in irritability, depression or feeling as if you're riding an emotional seesaw.

With Card 70, the more adaptable you are now, the easier and more quickly you can adjust to any ups and downs that might otherwise complicate your daily routine.

The Three of Pentacles

Whatever your situation, you can clearly see what will and will not work for you now. The Three of Pentacles can be particularly favorable for anyone who is about to launch a well-planned endeavor, or take an established job or relationship to the next level.

The more encouraging the situation, or other cards in the spread, the more direct and decisive your thought pattern and communication will be. This is a good time to conclude matters, projects or studies you've been working on because you can clearly see what will and will not work for you. You'll be more inclined to save than spend your money. You're also more efficient and creative. This is a good time to rear- range your circumstantial cupboards, because people will be dealing with the "real" you.

The more challenging the situation, or other cards in the spread, the more likely you may feel that what you have is holding you back from acquiring what you want or deserve – especially if your personal life has become cluttered with too many insecure or needy personalities. You may accuse someone else (or they may accuse you) of material or emotional misrepresentation. This isn't the time to start a new class, job or project because either you won't enjoy it or grasp the subject matter as quickly as you expected. Everyday travel may prove more to be more complex, costly and/or frustrating than usual.

At your best: now is an ideal time to call upon your strengths to conquer your weaknesses rather than disguise them. **However, should you be overstressed** or the Three of Pentacles appears in reverse, (upside down) beware a tendency to be too shortsighted, stubborn, or

Card 71
the Three of Pentacles

Subject Card Three is for thinking and networking.

Keywords:

Ambitious/ Thinking and Networking

For New Students:

Like the 3rd House in Astrology, our 3's signal news, ideas and activity that can keep us in-touch and on our toes, or lead us to change our mind at the last minute.

unforgiving. Should you feel that something is missing in your life, or seems to be undermining your ability to relax or, the quality of your performance (at work, home, or both) now is a good time to re-examine your goals.

Card 71 also favors everyone who is seeking a better way to build or rebuild their life.

The Four of Pentacles

Whether you've become too stingy or too free with your emotions, time or material resources, this is a reminder that no matter how hard you hope or try, you can't have matters both ways. The more stubborn you are now, the harder it will be to compromise with whatever changes are on your horizon, and the longer you will feel as if your back is to a wall.

The more encouraging the situation, or other cards in the spread, the more you're ready to "dig-in" and do whatever needs to be done – confident that you can handle come what may. This is a good time to cautiously explore any offers or possibilities that could lead to new or better employment. At work, home or both, you'll be perfectly content to take the time you need to complete matters to your specifications. Your realistic approach and handling of people and matters will bring you closer to people you care for and about.

The more challenging the situation, or other cards in the spread whether you had expected them to or not, other peoples' problems can become yours overnight. This may include the burden of caring for someone else. Your company or employer could encounter setbacks that pose a threat to your job security or income – or it may be time to come to grips with an emotional or medical issue of your own. Whatever your situation, allowing your frus- tration with any type of intrusion or the circumstances that caused them could handicap your desire to tend to matters as quickly as you should.

At your best: you can do your best work under pressure – from meeting deadlines that other people would consider impossible to pulling other people and ideas together in a manner that benefits everyone. **However, should you be overstressed** or the Four of Pentacles appears in reverse,

Card 72
the Four of Pentacles

Subject Card Four is all about your sense of belonging and security.

Keywords:

Ambitious/ Belonging and Security

For New Students:

Like the 4th House in Astrology, our 4's signal an increase or decrease in our material and domestic activities that could strengthen or disturb our sense of belonging.

(upside down) excessive self-awareness or self-concern can limit your objectivity and lead you to blow matters completely out of proportion. You may soon discover that whatever (or whoever) you're trying to hang onto is costing you more than it's worth.

Card 72 can denote self-inflicted burdens or problems that stem from trying too hard, whether you're trying too to avoid or accomplish something.

The Five of Pentacles

One or two matters will either not go your way or move as smoothly as you had hoped. Your emotional and material concerns may prove more complex, interwoven –or both. The greater your concerns, the greater your inner turmoil and the easier that turmoil could affect your better judgment, undermine your physical health or possibly trigger a freak accident or close call. The more in touch you are with your Faith, dreams or intuition the more easily you can make choices that are right for you.

The more encouraging the situation, or other cards in the spread, the more likely it is that one or two matters are either not going to go your way or move as smoothly as you had hoped. The good news is that they won't cost you as much time or money as they might have. You may even learn a valuable lesson through these matters, perhaps, about trying too hard. If you've been under too much pressure lately (self-induced or otherwise) this is a good time to "pamper" yourself as much as you can afford too. Should you presently be involved in charitable activities, you may earn some unexpected recognition for your generosity. The more challenging the situation, or other cards in the spread, the more likely you may feel as if everyone is simply too demanding – especially your loved ones, no matter what their age. Taking the slightest risk with your safety or finances could produce dire con- sequences. This is not the time to borrow or loan money. It may seem as if it's simply one delay after another in mat- ters. Everything about your work will become more chal- lenging and a little less enjoyable. Medically, your system may find it just as challenging to deal with a cure as an illness. Whatever your situation, remaining focused upon the "bigger picture" or the greater good will help you help yourself surmount these challenges more quickly.

Card 73
the Five of Pentacles

Subject Card Five is a card of conflict and speculation.

Keywords:

Ambitious/ Conflict and Speculation

For New Students:
Like the 5th House in Astrology, our 5's can also trigger an unexpected conflict of interest between our logic and emotions, in matters ranging from duty, to friendship, finance, romance - or parenting.

At your best: you can walk away from arguments that you could win – when you know the issue is pointless.
However, should you be overstressed or the Five of Pentacles appears in reverse, (upside down) you may blame your professional problems on your personal life and your personal problems on your professional life.

With Card 73, your emotional and material concerns are a little more complex because they are so interwoven.

The Six of Pentacles

From money, to time and opportunity, the Six of Pentacles reminds you waste not, want not. With the Six of Pentacles, the more con- fidence you have in your abilities, the easier you can attract the attention of people who can advance your interests. Although, "waste not, want not", should be your motto, you'd still be wise to carefully examine any and all opportunities that might come knocking at your door. If not, you could pay a higher price than you expected.

The more encouraging the situation, or other cards in the spread, you're going to tackle your daily routine with a renewed sense of vigor and purpose. A legal matter may soon be resolved in your favor. You may receive some type of bonus or recognition for a job well done. However, your determination to bring order into chaos wherever you go could be a double-edged sword if you overstep your bounds. You may become more conscious about your physical health, or change your sleeping habits to better accommodate your energy and work schedule. The more you hope to accomplish, the more you need to pace yourself, because you may also tire more quickly now. The more you hope to accomplish, the more you need to pace yourself, because you may tire more quickly now. You may become more conscientious about your physical health or change your sleeping habits to better accommodate your energy and work schedule.

The more challenging the situation, or other cards in the spread, your physical health or sleeping habits may suffer from nervous tension due to problems at work and/or at home. You may be reaping the consequences of your own, or someone else's finan- cial neglect, irresponsibility or immaturity. Whatever you're employment or routine, you're bound to wish you were doing something different. However, if you quit or lose your employ- ment now, it may be harder to find something new. Should you find new employment, settling in won't prove as easy as you had hoped. In a short while, you'll be able to use the lessons that you're learning the hard way now to help you chart a better path.

At your best: at work and at home, no detail is too small to escape your full attention. You can transform virtually any

Card 74
the Six of Pentacles

Subject Card Six represents commitment

Keywords:

Ambitious/ Commitment

For New Students:
Like the 6th House in Astrology, our 6's can also signal situations that can enhance or disrupt our peace of mind as we strive to keep pace with matters and people that comprise our daily routine.

task into an inspirational adventure. **However, should you be overstressed** or the Six of Pentacles appears in reverse, (upside down) faulty judgment may add additional complications to your financial and emotional network, or your determined approach may generate a little friction in some of your relationships.

With Card 74 The busier you are, the better you'll feel and the more you can accomplish for you, other people, and matters or foundations that are more deserving of your time, and efforts and generosity.

The Seven of Pentacles

Whatever the reason, you're about to take a closer look at endeavors and relationships into which you've been investing the majority of your time, money and emotions. So, whether or not your discoveries trigger a self-identity crisis, for better or worse some people are likely to encounter a different aspect of your personality. The less satisfied you are with your efforts the more challenging, it will be to continue to see only what you wish to be true. The more satisfied you are with the results of your labors, the less reluctant you will be to seek or accept new and better opportunities to expand your horizons.

The more encouraging the situation, or other cards in the spread, the more likely you and other people to gain a new sense of respect for one another. Your resourceful behavior and attitude will generate positive attention and perhaps some timely introductions to people that can benefit you. The busier you have to be, the more quickly you can conform to a more efficient behavior pattern, making it easier to clear away any and all clutter that is (or has been) standing in the way of your progress.

The more challenging the situation, or other cards in the spread, any negativity, resistance or confusion you encounter (no matter how small) could be "the last straw" that causes you to take your irritation out on other people. You could nurse a grievance or worry completely out of proportion especially (but not exclusively) if any aspect of a loved one's life or earning potential is in jeopardy.

At your best: your ability to remain focused on the positive and important aspects of any project or relationship now, can help prevent you from being overwhelmed by trivial concerns. **However, should you be overstressed,** or the Seven of Pentacles appears in reverse, (upside down) you may need to seriously consider seeking additional income

Card 75
the Seven of Pentacles

Subject Card Seven corresponds to your relationships.

Keywords:
Ambitious/ Relationships

For New Students: Like the 7ᵗʰ House in Astrology, our 7's can also signal an unexpected turn of events – for better or worse, concerning our relationships at work, home or both.

or reconstructing certain aspects of your relationships, at home, work, or both. The more challenging it is to confront or express your own feelings, the more quickly you can begin to expect the worst in matters, or imagine that other's are being untruthful or conspiring against you.

With Card 75 the more focused you are upon personal advancement, the easier and more quickly you can cut your losses and avoid recreating them. As an organizer, or mediator your resourceful strategies and positive attitude can make you an indispensable asset, at home, work – or both.

The Eight of Pentacles

The more comfortable you are with your abilities, the easier you can grasp "the big picture" in matters now and simply sort out the details as you go. Your recent achievements will speak for themselves and you as well! Whatever changes, challenges or obstacles you're about to confront now will only invigorate you and strengthen your determination to succeed. The less certain you are about what you want to have or do, the longer you may remain one of life's professional students – always claiming to know more than everyone else, but accomplishing less than anyone else.

The more encouraging the situation, or other cards in the spread, the more self-assertive and focused you will be upon what you want to achieve and what you need to do to make it happen! Everything that you deem a priority will receive your full attention and cooperation. Just be sure to provide an adequate explanation for postponing other matters. You'll want to devise ways to increase your material holdings. You may begin to play a more active role in guiding any current investments you have. You may consider taking a second job or explore self-employment. You may begin a private savings account or investment as a "just-in-case" measure. You may receive a promotion on your current job or begin to interview for a higher-paying position. You may also want to invest in your health and take confident steps towards preserving or improving it.

The more challenging the situation, or other cards in the spread, some type of emergency could either deplete your ready cash or threaten your savings account. You may begin to realize that the future of your job or company could be in jeopardy. You may begin a private savings account or investment as a "just-in-case" measure. A medical problem for yourself or someone close to you could prove to be more serious than you suspected. No matter how challenging the circumstances, take heart. Meeting these challenges is helping you transform former weaknesses into personal strengths.

At your best: you're a ready and willing worker with excellent powers of organization and leadership. No task is too large

Card 76
the Eight of Pentacles

Subject Card Eight stands for future renovation.

Keywords:

Ambitious/ Renovation

For New Students:
Like the 8th House in Astrology, our 8's can also provide clues concerning the stability of our future, with anyone or anthing that is important to us.

or too small to merit your full attention and concentration. **However, should you be overstressed** or the Eight of Pentacles appears in reverse, (upside down) you can become too focused upon petty grievances and resentments that limit rather than broaden your horizons. You may see self-gratification in any number of self-indulgences. What was once your "comfort-zone" may begin to feel more like a rut that is preventing you from making the most of yourself.

With Card 76, upon selecting your course of action you can become virtually immune to any threats or promises that encourage you to abandon your path. You're the perfect person to get a job done properly even if it takes more than one try.

The Nine of Pentacles

Personal achievement is your best means of attaining genuine peace of mind. As long as you understand that protecting your mate- rial resources is secondary to protecting yourself from self- delusions that can impede your better judgment, the Nine of Pentacles can be one of the most fortunate cards in the Tarot.

The more encouraging the situation, or other cards in the spread, the more benefits you stand to gain – thanks to your past perseverance and unwavering faith. You may discover that you have a secret admirer. You may receive a nomination, an award, reward, party, promotion or just sincere thanks and recognition at home, at work or from your community. Fam- ily or business connections could prove fortunate for you in some way. You may soon purchase, or inherit property. From finance to romance and everything in between (such as diet or health concerns, seeking a better job, redecorating your home – or updating your personal appearance) now's the time to stop "talking" about what you want to do and simply do it!

The more challenging the situation. or other cards in the spread, the more likely you are to hear news and gossip that is not only hard to believe but may be rather unkind or unfair to you as well! Think carefully before you retaliate, share secrets or pass along gossip or rumors because something you say now could come back to haunt you later. You are more likely to attract and be attracted by entertainments and people that could bring you more trouble, danger or heartache than they will be worth – especially (but not only) if you are grappling with some type of emotional disappointment or loss.

At your best: you possess great strength of character and pur- pose. You're as efficient as you are self-sufficient – able to enjoy others company and still be perfectly comfortable by yourself! **However, should you be overstressed,** or the

Card 77
the Nine of Pentacles

Subject Card
Nine represents your understanding.

Keywords:

Ambitious/
Understanding

For New Students:

Like the 9th House in Astrology, our 9's can also make it easier or more challenging to expand our outlook while maintaining our beliefs and self-confidence.

Nine of Pentacles appears in reverse, (upside down) the easier you can lull yourself into a false sense of security, the more you may need to be on guard against financial loss, material damage or perhaps even a threat to your reputation and integrity.

With Card 77, should you be expecting too much from matters or other people, or allowing them to demand too much from you, reality may soon puncture your fantasy. The stronger your determination to "get on with your life now" the sooner and easier you can transcend your former uncertainty, procrastina- tion or fear of rejection.

The Ten of Pentacles

This is all about feeling and taking a greater sense of responsibility towards other people and matters. Whether or not you feel either a little more romantic or nostalgic this week (and you may) you need to feel that the people you care for care about you and realize that you are always there for them.

The more encouraging the situation, or other cards in the spread, people who have more of what you want will motivate you to set your sights higher while those who have less will inspire you to count your blessings! You might get lucky playing the lottery with friends, family or co-workers. You will attract and be attracted to other people that are concerned about their future and you may discuss or share information about taxes, inheritance, insurance poli- cies and savings programs. If you are self-employed, it could be easier than you expected to branch out or sell your current business.

The more challenging the situation, or other cards in the spread, the more you may need to take better care of your physical health. You, or a loved one, could develop problems with or allergies to foods or conditions that never bothered you before. If you or a loved one has had an ongoing medical condition it could require more attention now. You may be required to take or share someone else's financial responsi- bility.. If you're not turned down for any type of credit or loan you may have to pay an exorbitant interest rate. Much to your chagrin, whatever the cause for the moment, economy will have to be your watchword.

At your best: your ability to radiate humor, peace and commonsense may make it almost impossible to determine where your friends begin and your family ends. **However, should you be overstressed**, or the Ten of Pentacles appears in reverse, (upside down) although you'd be wise to pay closer attention to the people and matters that mean the

**Card 78
the Ten of Pentacles**

**Subject Card Ten is a
card for Achievement.**

Keywords:

**Ambitious/
Achievement**

For New Students:
Like the 10th House in
Astrology, since our 10's
can also lead us to feel as
if we're closer to, or farther away from achiev-
ing our goals, they can
also make whatever
we're doing more or less
enjoyable.

most to you, beware of becoming so involved in others lives
that you lose track of your own affairs.

With Card 78, on some level, a link between your material
and circumstantial destiny with other people, at work and
home may soon be strengthened or weakened. For example: your employer may announce plans for future expansion or some other program that will stabilize your position,
or problems for your company or between you and your
employer could pose a threat to your employment.

CHAPTER 7

TIMING, NUMEROLOGY & DROPPED CARDS

Before we plunge into working with an actual Tarot spread, we need to discus two very important topics: Signature Cards and Timing.

SIGNATURE CARDS

I prefer to read without using a signature card, but please consider doing a few readings with them before you decide. The traditional Celtic Cross Tarot spread will require that you select a signature card. Our Tarot-Dynamic Celtic Cross does not. Signature cards are most often assigned in one of three ways – age, physical attributes or a corresponding astrological sign. AGE: While men that are at least eighteen years of age but under the twenty-five can be represented by the Knight that corresponds to their Astrological Sign, women that are at least eighteen but the age of twenty-five are generally represented by the Page that corresponds to their Astrological sign, and according to their gender, the King or Queen of Swords may be used to signify older people.

PHYSICAL ATTRIBUTES: In keeping with their gender while King or Queen of Cups can be used to represent people with blonde hair, people with red-hair may be symbolized by the King or Queen of Wands, and the King or Queen of Pentacles often signifies brunettes.

ASTROLOGICAL SIGNS: Astrologically, we each have our very own signature card. According to your gender, the signature card for the Fire Signs: Aries ♈, Leo ♌ or Sagittarius ♐ is the King or Queen of Wands. The signature card for the Earth Signs: Taurus ♉, Virgo ♍ and Capricorn ♑ is the King or Queen of Pentacles. The signature card for the Air Signs: Aquarius ♒, Gemini ♊ and Libra ♎ is the King and Queen of Swords. For the Water Signs: Scorpio ♏ Pisces ♓ and Cancer ♋, the signature card is the King of Queen of Cups.

When selecting a signature card, you can devise your own method, use the traditional selection, or even select a card from the Major Arcana if you wish. For instance, if you're reading for a woman who is hoping to become married you might select Card 19 (the Sun), or even Card 50 (the Ten of Cups), to represent her. Whereas, the King of Pentacles might be your choice to represent a businessman, the King of Swords could be used to signify a lawyer, Editor or Publisher.

TIMING EVENTS

Although timing events can be a challenge, every now and then one card will appear in several readings over the course of a year or for several different people in the space of a month. The more often one card is repeated in consecutive readings for a person the more valuable that card's definition is to their success or disappointment. In one reading it may represent a matter that they're grappling with, in another it may represent a matter they're avoiding. Each time it appears it will strike you differently, you'll receive and provide a little more insight about the situation. For example, early in 2001, my husband requested that I read his cards – a most infrequent occurrence. Card 73 the Five of Pentacles appeared in our overview when he cut the cards. It appeared that his employer was on the verge of making a poor decision. Three months later they sold the company. Six months later, my husband requested another Tarot reading. As is my custom we again used the Celtic Cross spread. Once again Card 73 the Five of Pentacles appeared, but this time it had travelled into the spread and was occupying the 3rd position, which represents the heart of the matter. Three weeks later he was laid off, but only for 3 months. Near the end of November 2002, my husband requested one more reading. The Five of Pentacles appeared yet again, but now it was in the 10th position (or outcome position) of the Celtic Cross. Shortly after New Year 2003, my husband was permanently laid off and within 8 more months the company itself, was no more. As they say, "Once is an occurrence, twice is a pattern, three times is a problem."

The more often one card is repeated throughout several readings for different people in the course of one week, month, or year the more likely it is that some sort of political, social or economic trend is either developing or under way in the world at large. In my experience this has happened twice, from early June of 2001 until September 11, 2001, and again from January 2008 until October 6, 2008.

As a rule, the more strongly I "feel" a matter in relation to a particular Tarot card, the sooner and more likely the event seems to come to pass. Eventually, you will "feel" this too. Bear in mind that I say, as a rule, and rules are made to be broken. Some time ago I did a series of what I felt were excellent – even inspired readings. I did not hear from the client again for a year and a half. When they contacted me they requested another reading as quickly as possible! After that urgent reading, they disclosed that they had enjoyed our previous sessions but were extremely disappointed when nothing that I had alluded to came to pass. However, they said, in the last week there been a sudden change for the worse at their place of employment. They then accidentally came across the recordings from our first two sessions. Hoping to take their mind off their troubles they played one tape after the other – and there I was describing in great detail exactly what had occurred and was happening *now*. Long ago I stopped trying to rationalize how that episode came to pass. It has happened a few times since with different clients, so hearing this may prove helpful to you.

TIMING AND THE MINOR ARCANA

There are also times when what we see and feel is as perplexing for us as it is for the person for whom we're reading. So, first of all be honest, let the person know that you cannot state a definite time frame with absolute certainty. Let's pretend you're doing a reading in mid May, which is the time of Taurus. Your puzzlement stems from a Wand in the Minor Arcana. Wands equal Fire Signs and times. The next time of fire would be Leo, which runs from the 23rd of July to the 23rd of August. After Leo, there won't be another Fire time until Sagittarius, which runs from November 23rd to the 21st of December. If the time period between now and Leo feels right, consider telling the person: "I feel this event will come to pass in between now Taurus, and Leo, July-August. If Leo doesn't "feel" right but you're not sure, consider telling them: "Although this could come to pass between now Taurus, and Leo, July-August, I'm more comfortable stating a time frame between Leo, July-August, and Sagittarius, November-December.

Should your timing dilemma stem from two cards within the same suit of the Minor Arcana, Cups for example, consider the following.   It's still Mid-May.   The next time of Water would be Cancer, after that comes Scorpio, then Pisces in the early portion of the next year.   Chances are good the event will come to pass between Cancer and Scorpio of this year, but if you're not comfortable making that pronouncement, expand your time frame saying: "Between Cancer June-July of this year and Pisces, February-March of next year".

BASIC TIMING GUIDE

Aries ♈ = Fire = Wands		March 21 to April 20
Taurus ♉ = Earth = Pentacles		April 21 to May 20
Gemini ♊ = Air = Swords		May 22 to June 21
Cancer ♋ = Water = Cups		June 22 to July 22
Leo ♌ = Fire = Wands		July 23 to August 23
Virgo ♍ = Earth = Pentacles		Aug. 24 to Sept. 22
Libra ♎ = Air = Swords		Sept. 23 to Oct. 23
Scorpio ♏ = Water = Cups		Oct. 24 to Nov. 22
Sagittarius ♐ = Fire = Wands		Nov. 23 to Dec. 21
Capricorn ♑ = Earth = Pentacles		Dec. 22 to Jan. 20
Aquarius ♒ = Air = Swords		Jan. 21 to Feb. 18
Pisces ♓ = Water = Cups		Feb. 19 to March 20

TIMING AND THE MAJOR ARCANA

In matters of timing Major Arcana cards can be particularly tricky. In most readings their role and nature is more spiritual or psychological than worldly. Whenever possible, I rely on Minor Arcana cards when timing events. However, there are those who prefer to read only the Major Arcana cards, and I can't say they're wrong if it works for them. For me, though, to perform a reading using only the Major Arcana Cards would be like reading half the story. There are many Tarot books available in bookstores and libraries. The majority of them contain remarkable — even lavish (though sometimes confusing) detail, especially concerning the Major Arcana. Most Major Arcana cards are purportedly ruled by a combination of two or more planets, and unfortunately, there are as many combinations as there are authors to devise them. So should you decide to use only your Major Arcana to perform a reading, my suggestion is to leave the timing to your intuition.

TIMING WITH THE TAROT AND NUMEROLOGY

This is one of the most reliable methods to improve the accuracy of your timing for legal, professional and financial matters, such as selling your home, professional mergers (or downsizing) or how soon you may expect an ongoing personal or legal matter to be resolved. Numbers are to Numerology[1] what the planets are to Astrology, and like the Astrologers, Numerologists have assigned individual characteristics to each number.

Until 1979, when Ms. Faith Javane and Ms. Dusty Bunker brought Numerology into the 20th Century with their book "Numerology and the Divine Triangle", Numerologists based their predictions, almost exclusively upon the properties of numbers one through nine. Date totals, were calculated by adding the month and the day together and then reducing the resulting number to a single digit.

For example: June 26th would be: $6 + 26 = 32$. $3 + 2 = 5$

Whether you arrived at the number 5 by way of numbers 14, 23, 32, 41 50, 59 68, 77 or any other combination[2] the Numerologist relied upon the characteristics associated with Number 5 to provide your forecast.

While working with the Rider-Waite Tarot Deck, Ms. Javane and Bunker, bent (if not broke) a Numerological taboo[3] once they realized that the individual Tarot definitions

---

[1] Numerology is the study of the symbolism of numbers, and their impact on the world as well as human behavior.

[2] including numbers that contain three or more digits.

[3] Throughout the ages, Numerologists credited Numbers 11, 22, 33 and 44 with enough strength to merit the tern "Master Numbers" which should never be broken down. Yet, one by one, Ms. Javane and Bunker did break them down – except for the Number 11, which governs cards, 29/11,38/11,47/11,56.11, 65/11 and 74/11 from the Minor Arcana.

for cards such as 32, (the Six of Wands) could finally enable Numerologists to clarify the personal differences between people who share the number 5 as a common denominator – just as Astrologers explain why (for instance) all Cancer Sun Signs neither think, react or behave in the same way.

For example, when reading number 32 as 32/5, the Tarot definition for Card 32 (Six of Wands) outlines the seekers aspiration, while the number 5 supplies their motivation and ability to attain that aspiration.

Including (rather than excluding) these additional properties for numbers such as 32 enabled Numerologists to blend the old with the new to increase the scope and clarity of *their* readings, and today virtually all Numerologists interpret and write double digits such as 32 as 32/5.

Now, by reading the bottom (or trigger) number for the designated outcome card in any tarot spread Tarot practitioners (like ourselves) can also determine whether and WHY the seeker can expect matters to unfold more slowly, or quickly.

Let's use the Aces for our example since they're the purest form of elemental energy and personal potential.

At its most basic level, Card 27, the Ace of Wands, is said to signal passionate changes and renewed energy, whereas Card 41, the Ace of Cups, allegedly heralds true love, pure joy and the gateway to Spiritual revelation, while Card 55, the Ace of Swords should invoke absolute triumph over adversity, and Card 69, the Ace of Pentacles ought to produce economic gains and losses of monumental proportions. Nonetheless, for every one miracle or major catastrophe that transpire after an Ace appears, there are even more instances when nothing special occurs. Yet, time after time after time, both Reader and Seeker blame faulty timing, when good tidings fail to materialize and credit divine intervention when bad news fails to manifest. Now let's see what happens with Tarot Dynamics.

Card 27/9 the Ace of Wands

$$27 = 2 + 7 = 9 \text{ or } 27/9$$

Wands: represent an opportunity or need to make or adapt to change.

From Chapter 3: "Circumstance, as well as your personal aspirations will force you to blaze your own trail through matters, in ways and at times when you least expect it".

From Chapter 2: 9 tests your beliefs and understanding in ways and at times that will surprise you, and crystallize your individuality to assist you in tying up whatever loose ends could be impeding your progress, as well as any you've been avoiding.

So with Card 27/9 the majority of changes often occur as a "quiet riot" – one or more, smaller incidents that trigger a simple and perhaps overdue, change in the Seekers perspective and understanding of a matter, people or, themselves.

Card 41/5 the Ace of Cups

4 + 1 = 5 or 41/5

Cups: represent your desire and ability to keep yourself and matters that give your life meaning flowing at an easy pace – or simply freeze everything in its tracks.

From Chapter 4: "By working more constructively now with your emotions, this time period can prove to be uncommonly productive and rewarding".

From Chapter 2: 5 is a "wild card" that can enable us to make the impossible-possible one moment, and trigger an unexpected conflict of interest between our logic and emotions, the next.

Card 41/5 seldom triggers as many happy beginnings and endings or as much personal enlightenment *as quickly* as we expect, because whatever their situation, the Seeker is presently more vulnerable to viewing matters from the best or worst standpoint of what they *want* to be true.

Card 55/1 the Ace of Swords

5 + 5 = 10. 1 + 0 = 1 or 55/1

Swords: challenge and ignite your intellect, as well as your desire to bring order into chaos, whether you are moving in the best or simply most convenient direction.

From Chapter 5: the Ace of Swords represents "a *possibility* of winning or losing more than you expect in matters."

Number 1: Like Card 1 the Magician the number 1 is synonymous with your survival instinct or desire to win – sometimes at any cost.

With Card 55/1, since our actions and reactions tend to be more instinctual or impulsive our crisis or reward tends to manifest sooner rather than later.

Card 69/6 the Ace of Pentacles

6 + 9 = 15. 1+5 = 6 or 69/6

Pentacles: indicate *reaping harvest*, as well as breaking new ground and planting new seeds in emotional *and* economic matters.

From Chapter 6: "An opportunity that could fall into your lap, or a dilemma could prove to be a blessing in disguise – possibly one of each!"

From Chapter 2: 6′ s often signal a time or opportunity to repair whatever needs to be fixed or clarified, whether in keeping with our daily routine, peace of mind or well-being.

This is why, shortly after Card 69/6 appears many people feel disappointed, or amazed by set-backs or a small problem that suddenly becomes more than they can handle. Yet even the Ace of Pentacles, frequently accompanies little things we must handle now, so we may tackle lager matters later, with greater success.

PUTTING NUMEROLOGY TO WORK WITH YOUR TAROT CARDS

When reading one or three Tarot cards for yourself, a quick consultation with the following guidelines will assist you in retaining your personal objectivity, and focus. Yet they are also the perfect companions for anyone who interprets designated outcome cards in larger tarot spreads, such as the Celtic Cross.

Whatever the situation, the trigger number will reveal whether and WHY you should expect matters to unfold more slowly, or quickly.

Whatever the situation, since outcome cards whose trigger Number are, 1, 4 or 7 inspire you to take an older matter to a new level or begin something new, matters tend to unfold or escalate more quickly.

Whatever the situation, with outcome cards whose trigger Number is, 2, 5, 8 or 11, no matter how urgent the situation, or how golden an opportunity; it is only smaller portions of a larger matter and picture that will evolve more slowly.

Whatever the situation, since outcome cards whose trigger Number is, 3, 6, or 9, are all about broadening your horizons more realistically, even the biggest changes often occur as a "quiet riot" – one or more smaller episodes that trigger a simple and perhaps overdue change, in your perspective and understanding.

WORKING WITH THE TAROT'S "TRIGGER" NUMBERS

The Number 1, which governs Card 1 the Magician, is also the force behind eight other Tarot Cards from the Major and Minor Arcana.

10/1 Fortune's Wheel	46/1 the Six of Cups
19/1 The Sun	55/1 Ace of Swords

28/1 Two of Wands   64/1 Ten of Swords

37/1 King of Cups   73/1 the Five of Pentacles

The Number 1, which governs Card 1 the Magician also triggers eight other Tarot Cards from the Major and Minor Arcana. Just like Card 1 the Magician, your willingness or refusal to apply your will power constructively, is what will reward or undermine your efforts. Whatever the situation, since your primary motivation or biggest challenge, will be to take an older matter to the next level or beginning something new, matters will unfold or escalate more quickly – which may cause you to feel more or less confident about trusting your judgment, or become a point of reference that you look back upon and say "where I am now, stems from the day I decided to do (or say) that."

The Number 2, which governs Card 2 the High Priestess, is also the force behind two other Tarot Cards – both from the Major Arcana.

11/2 Justice   20/2 Judgment

2's are all about your level of attachment to people and matters, which depends upon how much you feel you are receiving in return – whether from your family, friends, employer, material investments – even a course of study or medical treatment. Yet, no matter how urgent the situation, or how golden an opportunity, it is only smaller portions of a larger matter and picture that will evolve more slowly, and require more time and effort, to be perfected, understood, appreciated or resolved.

The Number 3, which governs Card 3 the Empress is also the force behind eight more Tarot Cards from the Major and Minor Arcana.

12/3 Hanged Man   48/3 Eight of Cups

21/3 World   57/3 Three of Swords

30/3 Four of Wands   66/3 Queen of Pentacles

39/3 Knight of Cups   75/3 Seven of Pentacles

Whether from the Major or Minor Arcana 3s are all about your level of rationalization – how much and how well you absorb and react to whatever is happening to you and around you, from get-togethers to emergencies. So from Card 3 the Empress to 75/3 the Seven of Pentacles it's all about broadening your horizons, more realistically, the majority of changes often occur as a "quiet-riot" – one or more smaller episodes that trigger a simple change in your perspective.

The Number 4, which governs Card 4 the Emperor, is also the force behind another eight Tarot Cards from the Major and Minor Arcana.

13/4 Death	49/4 Nine of Cups
22/4 Fool	58/4 Four of Swords
31/4 Five of Wands	67/4 Knight of Pentacles
40/4 Page of Cups	76/4 Eight of Pentacles

Whether from the Major or Minor Arcana, 4's correspond to your sense of personal security and belonging. Whatever the situation, since your primary motivation or biggest challenge will be to take an older matter to a new level or begin something new, matters will unfold or escalate more quickly. So from Card 4 the Emperor to Card 76/4 the Eight of Pentacles, whether the 4 is signaling a control issue or simply an increase in your usual concerns, the stronger your sense of belonging the more quickly and easily your drive for security will enable you to begin, complete or resolve matters, as well as any outstanding differences more easily.

The Number 5, which governs Card 5 the Hierophant, is also the force behind eight other Tarot Cards from the Major and Minor Arcana.

14/5 Temperance	50/5 Ten of Cups
23/5 King of Wands	59/5 Five of Swords

32/5 Six of Wands	68/5 Page of Pentacles
41/5 Ace of Cups	77/5 Nine of Pentacles

Whether from the Major or Minor Arcana, 5's are "wildcards", that can either help you make the impossible - possible or trigger a conflict of interest between your logic and emotions. So, no matter what the situation or how golden the opportunity; it's only a smaller portion of the bigger picture, which will evolve more slowly. So from Card 5 the Hierophant to Card 77/5 the Nine of Pentacles, matters tend to unfold more dramatically, than quickly. Whether due to anticipation, aggravation or anxiety, the Seeker is in a more vulnerable time period or frame of mind when it's easier to believe or more desirable to see and act upon whatever you want to be true.

The Number 6, which governs Card 6 the Lovers, is also the force behind eight more Tarot Cards from the Major and Minor Arcana.

15/6 the Devil	51/6 King of Swords
24/6 Queen of Wands	60/6 Six of Swords
33/6 Seven of Wands	69/6 Ace of Pentacles
42/6 Two of Cups	78/6 Ten of Pentacles

Whether from the Major or Minor Arcana 6's are all about repairing whatever needs to be repaired or clarified to handle your commitments more efficiently. So from Card 6 the Lovers to 78/6 the Ten of Pentacles since 6's are more concerned with broadening your horizons, more realistically, the majority of changes often occur as a "quiet-riot" – one or more smaller episodes that trigger a simple change in your perspective. Perhaps that's why, from Card 6 the Lovers to Card 78/6 the Ten of Pentacles many matters also tend to unfold in stages much like a two or three act play.

The Number 7, which governs Card 7 the Chariot, is also the force behind only seven other Tarot Cards from the Major and Minor Arcana.

16/7 Tower   34/7 Eight of Wands

25/7 Knight of Wands   43/7 Three of Cups

52/7 Queen of Swords   70/7 Two of Pentacles

61/7 Seven of Swords

Whether from the Major or Minor Arcana 7's are all about the constructive or self-defeating manner in which you handle (or allow yourself to be handled) in your personal and professional relationships. Since your primary motivation or biggest challenge will be to take an older matter to a new level or begin something new, matters will unfold or escalate more quickly. So from Card 7 the Chariot to Card 70/7, the Two of Pentacles, whether the Seeker encounters an opportunity, complication, obligation or request matters will tend to develop more rapidly.

The Number 8, which governs Card 8 Strength, is the force behind seven more Tarot Cards from the Major and Minor Arcana.

17/8 Star   53/8 Knight of Swords

26/8 Page of Wands   62/8 Eight of Swords

35/8 Nine of Wands   71/8 Three of Pentacles

44/8 Four of Cups

Whether from the Major or Minor Arcana, 8s are all about opportunities and situations that have changed, or could change your life. They often provide clues about your future with anything or anyone that is valuable to you, such as, your relationships, source of income, health, and the health or prosperity of those you care for. So from Card 8 Strength to Card 71/8 the Three of Pentacles, whatever the situation it's only a smaller portion of the bigger picture, and despite whatever steps you need, to take now, the complete picture will tend to unfold more slowly.

The Number 9, which governs Card 9 the Hermit, is also the force behind seven other Tarot Cards from the Major and Minor Arcana.

18/9 Moon	54/9 Page of Swords
27/9 Ace of Wands	63/9 Nine of Swords
36/9 Ten of Wands	72/9 Four of Pentacles
45/9 Five of Cups	

Whether from the Major or Minor Arcana, 9s test and/or reward your beliefs, values and understanding – in ways, and at times that often surprise you and crystallize your individuality. So from Card 9 the Hermit to 72/9 the Four of Pentacles, since broadening your horizons more realistically, is the bottom-line whether you're hoping to sell or purchase something of significance, mend, end or finalize an agreement, you're more likely to obtain your objective in a manner that also alters your perspective.

The Number 11,which governs card 11 Justice is also the force behind our last six Tarot Cards, all of which come from the Minor Arcana.

29/11 Three of Wands	56/11 Two of Swords
38/11 Queen of Cups	65/11 King of Pentacles
47/11 Seven of Cups	74/11 Six of Pentacles

Like Card 11 Justice, the Number 11, corresponds to personal insight and inspiration whether to assist you in uniting other people to reach a common goal, cope with changes that you encounter or create, or devise some better way to obtain your fair share in matters. Yet, no matter how urgent the situation or how golden the opportunity, it's only a smaller portion of the bigger picture, which will evolve more slowly. So From Card 29/11 the Three of Wands to Card 74/11 the Six of Pentacles, although matters tend to erupt more quickly they will unfold or be resolved more slowly.

To demonstrate how naturally and easily Numerology and the Tarot can work can together we'll be using the example of a Three Card and Celtic Cross Spread.

3 CARD SPREAD
Outcome Card: Card 30/3, the Four of Wands.

Keywords: Changeable/Incentive & Security.

Wands: represent an opportunity or need whether to make or adapt to change.

Whether from the Major or Minor Arcana 3s are all about your level of rationalization – how much and how well you absorb and react to whatever is happening to you and around you.

So no matter how encouraging or challenging Cards One and Two may be, since the motivational (or trigger) number is a 3, whether you'll be dealing with unexpected news, or taking action concerning a problem matters will also unfold in a way that will broaden your horizons, perspective, or both more realistically.

| State of affairs | Self | Challenges |
| (Hindsight) | (Insight) | (Foresight) |

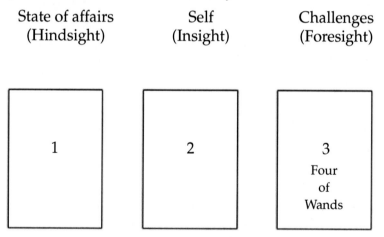

Please Note: Interpreting the trigger number for all 3 cards may provide more personal enlightenment than you're prepared for, unless your objectivity is in high gear.

TRADITIONAL CELTIC CROSS SPREAD

With the Celtic Cross the 10th Tarot Card, represented by Card 76/4 the Eight of Pentacles is the "official", outcome card. Pentacles signal economic and emotional concerns, while eights pertain to opportunities and situations that have, or could change your life. Assuming that the situation and other cards could presently go either way, by reading Card 76 as 76/4 it would be in the Seeker's best interest inform them that although matters will begin unfolding more rapidly in the near future, they will also reveal additional clues and factors that the Seeker should seriously consider before deciding whether or not to sign a formal agreement.

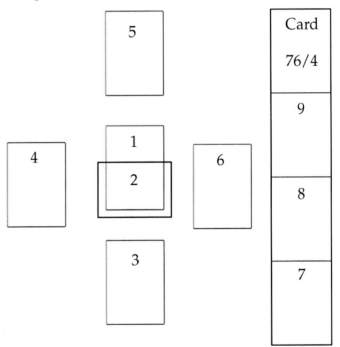

When working with the Celtic Cross, although the 10th Tarot Card is the "official" designated outcome card, there are no hard and fast rules. Many years ago I began reading the 5th and 10th Tarot cards together as my designated outcome cards – simply because they work best for my readings.

However, when dealing with seekers whose history consists of more potential and opportunity than confidence, or; whose "comfort-zone" is changing through matters beyond their control, reading the trigger numbers for the 1st and 10th Tarot Cards in the Celtic Cross can enable you to determine whether the seeker is more or less prepared to deal with the outcome – if they choose to let matters lie, or move on in life.

PLEASE NOTE: Attempting to interpret the bottom number for all 10 cards WILL prove more hazardous than helpful in to maintaining your focus *and* intuitive clarity.

FALLEN CARDS: "WHAT FALLS TO THE FLOOR COMES TO THE DOOR"

Every now and then, even the most relaxed Seeker will drop one, two or even three Tarot cards at one time, while shuffling the deck. Anytime this occurs, it's as if the cards are assisting the seeker in "covering all their bases", because whether the Seeker drops, one, two or three cards at one time, they can then receive two readings at once – one that relates to the fallen cards, plus the full reading yet to come!

My first experience with "dropped, or fallen cards" came about one day in the Tea Room, as I was beginning to develop my clientele. While shuffling, the seeker dropped two cards on the floor. Upon retrieving them, they asked "what shall I do?" to which I replied, "just replace them in the deck, and continue shuffling until you feel ready to stop."

We then went on to have a very good session, but after the seeker said goodbye, one of our more experienced readers made her way to my table, smiled, and said "Anna, what falls to the floor, comes to the door." Realizing that I had no idea what she meant, she kindly explained to me, what I am sharing with you today, along with a Tarot-Dynamics twist!

When a fallen Tarot card lands face up, within a matter of hours or days (not weeks) some type of test or reward, in relation to the cards definition, will come to pass, concerning a matter or person that is presently not on the your mind – or likely to appear in your full reading! For example: While shuffling the cards, the Seeker drops Card 7 the Chariot face up. After laying out the entire spread the full reading appears to be focused upon a concern about the Seeker 's employment-which could also relate to the Chariot. Then, within the next three days, you receive a call from the Seeker stating that you were correct about their job issue, but they also just incurred a major car repair that apparently came from out of the blue! Or did it? In Chapter 1 concerning the Chariot, "Tarot Dynamics" states that, "issues relating to travel as well as communication, could soon find you revising your personal, professional and financial strategies and schedules."

When a fallen Tarot card land face down, (meaning that you cannot see the illustration) the event tends to be farther away. The more positive the definition, the more likely that the Seeker is or soon can be on the right path to bring the event to fruition. Again, using the Seekers car as an example, a more positive aspect of Card 7 the Chariot falling face down is that, there could be "a romantic, adventurous or unusual story behind what brings bring the Seeker a better automobile. The more challenging the definition, the more likely the Seeker can minimize if not completely avoid an upset by changing course or taking action now. In this instance, whether or not the Seeker has been "nursing" their present car, "Tarot Dynamics" says, "your patience is sure to be tested", in this case by "annoying mechanical breakdowns." However it also says that, "confronting the worst in matters now, no matter how reluctantly, can help free the best in you." So, the next time you see the Seeker, they may say "less than a month after our last session, my car began needing one repair after another. Last week, I'd finally had enough and took a part-time job to help pay for a better car!

Another advantage, to reading cards that have fallen or dropped to floor, is that they help to minimize those times, when in recalling your last session, although many matters *did* come to pass, you and the Seeker were taken by surprise concerning another issue you didn't expect.

I choose to interpret "fallen cards', before I conduct the Seekers full reading, simply because they impress me, as someone saying "before you begin – you need to know". However, that is *my* preference, so please, allow *your* intuition, to guide you in determining whether to read them before or after you conduct the full reading.

Whether face-up or down, Major Arcana Cards signal an unexpected development, which will trigger a turning point, in the Seeker 's perception of a matter, or person, that is presently NOT on the seekers mind or likely to appear in todays full reading.

For Example: The Seeker has dropped Card 8 Strength. Since their main concern is to sell their house, Strength might suggest that selling the house could take a bit longer. Yet, two weeks later, the Seeker calls you in great distress, because they just discovered that their best friend of many years is not and has not been a true friend. While the issue of friendship never appeared in the reading, clearly the Seeker now needs some additional Strength to see them through this unexpected episode.

Should the Seeker drop Card 1 the Magician, a sudden turn of events will require them to devise a new strategy for taking charge of matters, or withstanding a challenge.

Should the Seeker drop *any* Major Arcana Card, ranging from Card 11 Justice to Card 22 the Fool, aside from whatever definition you assign to the card, its personal strength is more likely to be tested than rewarded, due to a concern that may temporarily prove more significant than the full reading yet to come.

For Example: The Seeker has dropped Card 20, Judgment, whose Personal Strength is Patience. Yet, the Seeker received a tremendously positive reading from cards that figuratively forecast imminent bliss. Yet, next week the Seeker calls you, and they are quite annoyed. Two days after their session everything, at work and home, began to go wrong and it hasn't stopped yet! Does this mean that your reading was totally incorrect? Maybe yes, maybe no, but Judgment clearly indicated that the Seeker's patience would be tested whether before or after they could claim their prize.

Dropping any Subject Card (Numbers 2-10) whether from the Wands, Cups, Swords or Pentacles, will signify a situation, opportunity, mood or obstacle (in keeping with its suit) that will come out of nowhere and could pass just as quickly as tempest in a tea pot – as long as the Seeker can avoid making a mountain out of a molehill.

While Court Cards, (he King, Queen, Knight, Page or Ace) will occasionally signal an unexpected bit of news from, or about a relative or an authority figure, they will always signify a fresh burst of personal energy, or inspiration connected to a matter, or person that is presently not on the Seeker's mind – or likely to appear in today's full reading.

ABOUT TAROT SPREADS

In todays world there are more Tarot spreads than questions. By simply, "Googling" Tarot Spreads, you can find any number of Tarot Web Sites that offer at *least* three different Tarot spreads that will allegedly answer every possible question concerning love, money, health or happiness.

To name a few, there are:

Tarot Spreads

Tarot Spreads for Beginners

Tarot Spreads Relationship

Tarot Spreads Love

Tarot Spreads Yes or No

Tarot Spreads Future

That's a *lot*. However, the Tarot is like anything else – the longer you work with it, the more proficient you'll become. So please take some time to experiment with different Tarot spreads, as well as devising your own Tarot spreads. Yet no matter how exciting this may sound, you also need to know that whatever type of Tarot spread you choose to read is secondary to your skill as a reader. Since a truly adept Tarot reader, is also "in sync" with their intuition, they can often obtain just as much accurate information from reading just one Tarot card as when they read two or more.

CHAPTER 8

TAROT DYNAMICS IN ACTION

THE ONE CARD SPREAD–PERSONAL GUIDANCE

This simple technique is an excellent method for reducing stress, enhancing your focus, and enabling you to see the "big" picture in matters. This technique can be particularly enlightening if you perform it during your favorite part of the day, whether you're a morning person, daytimer or a night owl. If you've recently been feeling irritable or restless for no real reason, separating the Major Arcana cards from your Tarot deck and selecting a card from the Major Arcana may help you discover what your inner-self is trying to tell you. However, if you're seeking spiritual reinforcement because your life is going well, somewhat unsettling, or simply going nowhere, using the entire Tarot deck is the best idea. People who choose to start each day by drawing and interpreting one card from their entire Tarot Deck, much like reading your horoscope, refer to it as their Card Of The Day aka. C.O.T.D.

Whatever your reason, relax. Take your time. Shuffle your cards in any manner you wish, while concentrating upon a place or activity that you enjoy, such as walking along a beach or through a forest. When you're ready, fan your cards across the tabletop and select one from anywhere in the deck, but before doing so study them for a moment. Although you may use either hand to select your card, consider using your left hand as it is closest to your heart.

Let your hand drift above all the cards before making your choice. When you do this, don't be surprised if you're eye or your hand feels drawn to one particular section of the cards. If so, it's perfectly normal and you will probably make your selection from there. However, it's also perfectly normal if you don't always feel an attraction to one particular card or section of cards. Remove the card of your choice from the deck and place it face up in front of you. If it appears upside down please place it right side up.

This card's definition offers suggestions to help you handle yourself and matters.

If you've selected a card from the:

Major Arcana: = personal transformation. The matters you're grappling with are karmic in origin. This cards definition offers suggestions that can replenish your peace of mind.

Wand: = Change. This cards definition offers suggestions that can assist you in making or adapting to changes more easily. It may even help you avoid making hasty changes that you could regret.

Cup: = Emotion. This cards definition offers suggestions that can heighten your awareness, enrich your creativity or help prevent your emotions or imagination from running away with you.

Sword: = Challenge. This cards definition offers suggestions that can replenish your courage and determination.

Pentacle: = Ambition. This cards definition offers suggestions that can help you increase or re-establish your security. It may also help you minimize or withstand a material dilemma.

THE THREE CARD SPREAD: PERSONAL ENLIGHTENMENT

Whenever I feel the need to read my own cards, this is my favorite spread. Why? Because it tells me what I need to know and can do – without jeopardizing my objectivity. If your concerns revolve around your inner-self, whether reaffirming your self-control or a question about your health you may wish to read for yourself using only the cards from the Major Arcana. However when other matters and questions prompt you to seek spiritual reinforcement, use your entire deck of Tarot cards.

Ready? We're going to repeat the same procedure that we used to select one card. Relax. Take your time. Shuffle your cards in any manner you wish while concentrating upon a place or activity that you enjoy, such as walking along a beach or through a forest. When you're ready, fan your cards across the tabletop, selecting three cards from anywhere in the deck, but before doing so study them for moment. Let your left hand drift above all the cards before making your choice. Remember it's perfectly normal if you're eye or your hand sometimes feels drawn to one particular section of the cards and it's normal if you don't always feel a particular attraction to any one section of cards. Remove the cards of your choice from the deck and place them face up in front of you. If it appears upside down please place it right side up.

State of affairs (Hindsight)	Self (Insight)	Challenges (Foresight)
1	2	3

Now before you begin to retrieve each cards definition, study the cards, recall our formula and see what "feelings" you receive from the cards you selected.

MAJOR ARCANA CARDS = Personal Transformation. Major Arcana Cards test, reward, and replenish your strength of character.

WANDS = Change. Wands can promote changes that lead to personal renewal by helping you accept the necessity of making some changes and adapt to others.

CUPS = Emotion. Cups signify whether your desire and ability to believe in and work towards a brighter tomorrow is a little stronger or weaker now.

SWORDS = Challenge. Self-control can transform the ideas and challenges that you initiate as well as encounter into an opportunity to succeed.

PENTACLES = Ambition. Pentacles are most often associated with financial and professional advancement, material acquisition, material rewards and/or material crisis.

TAROT DYNAMICS AND THE CELTIC CROSS

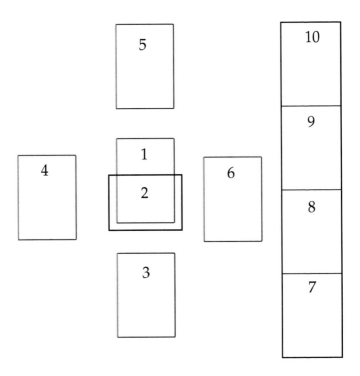

The Celtic cross may be the best-known and most popular of all the Tarot spreads. It is an excellent spread with which to do a reading for someone else. Once you become more familiar with your Tarot cards, and more confident about interpreting them, the Seeker may not need to ask their question out loud. For now, however, allowing the seeker to ask you what they wish to know will help you remain focused and allow you to see more of what they need to know. Simple questions are best. For example, "I've been concerned about a work matter", or "I'm hoping to move", or even "How's my love life?" Invite them to ask one question. If you don't, they may produce a list, which would intimidate even the most adept Tarot reader. The less they say, the less inhibited you'll feel and the more you'll see in their cards.

Let them ask their question before they begin to shuffle the cards. If you're using a signature card please select it from the deck after the seeker asks their question and before they begin to shuffle the cards. Place it right side up on the table facing you, in the position of Card number 1 and focus on the seekers signature card while they relax, think pleasant thoughts and shuffle the rest of the deck. If you are not using a signature card, the card that will occupy the first position will provide helpful clues concerning whatever the seeker needs to know. Either way, ask the seeker to relax and think pleasant thoughts while shuffling the cards. Encourage them to take their time and shuffle the cards in any manner they wish until they feel ready for you to read them.

When the Seeker is ready, you may begin to lay out the cards according to the diagram. Let the story that you have to tell them flow naturally. Take your time. Their question may have been about purchasing a new car, but you're going to see much more than a black and white yes or no. You may, for example, also see a new job, a promotion, a residence change or unexpected company arriving. Although they may be planning on purchasing that new car next week, you may see and sense a delay – whether an unexpected bill or the fact that they can't comfortably afford the purchase right now. Tell them what you see and feel through the cards. You may not always be able to tell people what they want to hear, but you'll always be able to tell them what they need to know. Many times people are merely seeking unbiased affirmation of something they already know.

Don't be afraid to let them record your session. One or more things that you say today that they can't immediately relate to are likely to become perfectly clear in a matter of weeks or a couple of months.

Here is a placement and referral guide to the Celtic Cross to help you get started.

The prompts for Card Number 1 contain more detail than the prompts for Cards 2-10 because:

Card Number 1 suggests the Seeker's reasons for having the reading.

Major Arcana: You are in a period of personal transformation and self-awareness.

Wand: You have been encountering many changes in matters and people lately.

Wand Court Card: You are, or are about to become more self-assertive and may be luckier than you realize, if you don't become too overconfident.

Wand Subject Card: You have been contemplating the wisdom of making some changes.

Cup: You have been more emotional and/or reflective lately.

Cup Court Card: Your feelings and intuition are more intense now. Whether for better or worse, your feelings are altering your emotional perspective and behavior.

Cup Subject Card: You're daydreaming, wishing, hoping, wanting to know but afraid to ask where matters are going.

Sword: You are, or will need to become more focused upon an important matter.

Sword Court Card: You are in a state of fluctuation. One moment you believe you can't lose; the next you believe you can't win. Even so, you are very determined, whether to pursue a new goal or finalize an old one.

Sword Subject Card: You are at a crossroads about how to best handle a person or situation.

Pentacle: You are concerned about your material stability or emotional security – maybe both.

Pentacle Court Card: Emotionally, materially or both you are striving to put down new roots.

Pentacle Subject Card: You need to consider weeding your circumstantial garden. Some matters need more sun; others need more shade.

Card Number 2 states why it's likely to be a little easier or more challenging for the seeker to handle what comes successfully.

Major Arcana: The upcoming matters are karmic. The happier you are with yourself now the more quickly and surely you will resolve any problems that could arise. The less satisfied you are with yourself or your life now the longer matters will remain in limbo until you are willing to consider an alternative course of action.

Wand: Matters may prove more challenging but meeting them will cause you to feel more alive. Flexibility is the key to making the most or best of whatever changes you set in motion as well as any that could take you by surprise.

Cup: The stronger your emotional objectivity the more accurate your intuition, so the sooner you will recognize the "bigger picture" and the less likely you are to fool yourself or be fooled by others.

Sword: much will depend upon your frame of mind. The greater your determination to succeed the sooner you will transform potential stumbling blocks into stepping-stones. The longer you choose to remain focused on the problem instead of seeking a logical solution the longer you will remain a victim of circumstance.

Pentacle: The upcoming matters will provide opportunities for you to reap some rewards, while tackling some additional or overdue duties and responsibilities. The more focused you are upon getting ahead in life the right way the less wasteful you will be with your time and resources.

Card Number 3 outlines the heart of the matter; where the seeker stands or what they need to know more about.

Major Arcana: you are at a turning point concerning your past and future goals.

Wand: approaching changes at home, at work or both.

Cup: emotional concerns.

Sword: tension or instability at home, at work, or both.

Pentacle: concerns about your personal and professional status and ambitions.

Card Number 4 suggests that either a past event or a personal habit that could be influencing the seeker's present concerns or behavior.

Major Arcana: you've been feeling yourself and your life changing in ways that you didn't expect. Perhaps you believe you've received a circumstantial wake-up call. Then too, maybe peace of mind has always seemed to elude you.

Wand: a desire to broaden your horizons or put more distance between yourself and matters (or people) that you can see will never change. Or, perhaps you have always feared rather than welcomed change – except on your terms.

Cup: Happy or sad recollections that have been causing your imagination to run away with you lately. Then too, perhaps viewing people and matters, as you want to see them instead of as they really are has always posed a problem.

Sword: the circumstances, under which a cause or goal was won or lost. Or, perhaps, a tendency leap before you look may simply be a habitual part of your behavior.

Pentacle: a recent increase or decrease, in your job status or material holdings may be spurring your drive for advancement. Then to, sound money management may have always posed a problem for you.

Card Number 5 suggests what the seeker could achieve but also needs to beware of.

Major Arcana: Achieve Truth. Beware Self-Doubt

Wand: Achieve Self-renewal, flexibility and independence. Beware Personal burn out

Cup: Achieve Peace of mind. Beware Procrastination

Sword: Achieve Inspiration and self-control. Beware Self-righteousness

Pentacle: Achieve Greater opportunity. Beware scattering your energies and wasting your resources.

Card Number 6 outlines conditions and matters in the near future.

Major Arcana: events at work or at home will test your character

Wand: sudden gains or opposition may come from nowhere

Cup: your emotions

Sword: stress

Pentacle: time for a reality check

Card Number 7 outlines conditions and matters that could complicate the heart of the matter.

Major Arcana: concern about failure, mediocrity

Wand: inability to make or cope with change

Cup: disappointment, loneliness or preoccupation with the past.

Sword: opposition or retribution.

Pentacle: loss of security or reputation

Card Number 8 outlines what the seeker stands to learn or gain in the near future.

Major Arcana: understanding, enlightenment

Wand: happiness

Cup: peace of mind

Sword: courage

Pentacle: security

Card Number 9 suggests the type of impact that the seeker's interactions with other people can have upon the situation.

Major Arcana: independence, confidence and constructive self-assertion.

Wand: the opportunity to branch out and become more resourceful.

Cup: new awareness and appreciation of yourself and others.

Sword: more constructive self-expression and effective bargaining techniques.

Pentacle: stability and resolution; to know where you stand in matters.

Card 10 presents the bottom line for the entire reading

Remember: a more challenging outcome card simply means you have a little more work ahead.

Major Arcana: you're ending an old chapter and entering a new phase in life.

Wand: you're on the brink of a very active, and adventurous if somewhat hectic time period.

Cup: you're undergoing an emotional and possibly spiritual transformation.

Sword: your greatest challenge will be to remain focused upon your ultimate goal.

Pentacle: Approach the future optimistically yet, realistically.

CHAPTER 9

MAJORITIES

Now we are going to address and answer the age old question of which cards in a Celtic Cross Spread are the most important. Here are five pertinent examples and comprehensive guidelines that can transform a "good" reading into "great" reading.

Example One

Upon looking at the complete layout you see that three out of ten cards are Kings. According to Chapter Two, "the more Kings there are in the spread the more important your past and present relationships with men or authority figures will be to your progress". This indicates that whether or not you'd expected to, you're likely to hear from, about, or be in contact with more men than usual for whatever reason. No matter what cards accompany those three Kings, they are the focal point of the reading and whatever your gender your initiative is about to receive a boost – whether to set new wheels in motion or resolve an ongoing situation. The other cards will reveal more of what you need to know concerning the nature or outcome of this contact. Three or more of ANY identical Court Card (3 Kings, Queens, 3 Knights, 3 Pages, 3 Aces) constitutes a majority.

Example Two

Upon looking at the complete layout you see that five out of ten cards are from the Major Arcana. According to "Chapter 1 " the more Major Arcana Cards there are in the spread the more emotionally or spiritually significant this reading will prove to be". This indicates that the Seeker is at, or approaching, some type of turning point. No matter what cards accompany those five Major Arcana Cards, they are the focal point of the reading. Each of their personal strengths represent something that can assist the Seeker and prevent them from becoming overwhelmed by one or while one or more their weaknesses. The other cards will reveal more of what you need to know concerning the Seekers situation, or the reasons for it – possibly both.

Five or more of *any* Major Arcana Cards (Numbers 1–22) constitutes a majority.

Example Three

Upon looking at the complete layout you see that six out of ten cards are Sword subject cards. According to Chapter Five, "If the majority of the spread consists of Swords, your greatest challenge will be to remain focused upon your ultimate goal". This indicates that the Seeker is either in the midst of, or about to encounter a distracting situation. No matter what cards accompany those Swords, the situation they outline are the focal point of the reading, while the four remaining cards will reveal more of what the seeker needs to know concerning the reasons for this delay or distraction as well as their options for expediting the situation. Three or more of *any* Subject Cards from the same suit constitutes a majority.

Example Four

Now let's mix-n-match. Upon looking at the complete layout you see that three out of ten cards are Subject Number 5 cards. According to Chapter 2 "the more fives you find throughout your reading, the more adversity or temptation you are about to confront, so the more you may need to rely upon your originality, creativity and flexibility". You also see that three out of the remaining seven cards are Cups. According to Chapter 3, "if the majority of the spread consists of Cups, the matters at hand may prove to be more complex than they appear, or your manner of handling them may be more emotional than the matter itself." So no matter what cards accompany those three 5's and three Cup cards, together they form the focal point of the reading. The cards that accompany those 6 cards will reveal more of what you need to know concerning the situation.

Six or more of any combination (3 and 3) constitutes a majority.

Example Five

Occasionally, the first card (which represents the seeker) and the last card (which represents the outcome) will be from the same suit and the only representatives of that suit. No matter what the suit it will take longer for the Seekers concerns to be resolved to the Seekers satisfaction. Should the first and last card be the only representatives from the:

Major Arcana; matters may not be completely resolved for a year or longer.

Minor Arcana; whether or not the seeker is aware of it they are about to embark upon a very tumultuous time-period in accordance to the basic keyword for the suit itself.

Example Six

Should the first and last cards each be a subject cards pay attention to their numbers as well. For instance, readings that begins with:

Card 30 the Four of Wands and ends with Card 31 the Five of Wands could indicate a particularly busy and possibly quarrelsome time period at work, home or both.

Card 42 the Two of Cups and ends with Card 50 the Ten of Cups could indicate that a proposal of marriage, or a child or even a new home is on the way. However, depending upon the accompanying cards, it could also indicate reconciliation after a misunderstanding or meeting someone completely new.

Card 57 the Three of Swords and ends with Card 51 the King of Swords could indicate loss of a job that may lead to a better position with a better employer or even self-employment. Then too, some type of disagreement could result in legal action or consulting a specialist may avert a serious medical issue.

Card 76 the Eight of Pentacles and ends with Card 70 the Two of Pentacles could indicate that the seeker is not as materially astute as they imagine. Whatever they are hoping for may not materialize as quickly as they hope, expect or deserve.

Whatever the situation, encourage the seeker consult the cards again in about 3 months.

In my experience, an easier or more "encouraging" reading consists of a wide variety of suits and numbers. The more times one particular suit or number is repeated the more "challenging" the circumstance they represent and the more significant that circumstance will be to the Seekers future. Do not mistake the word "challenge" for "catastrophe". More often than not, the term "challenge" simply refers to a busier or more active time period, or a matter whose resolution may require more time. Being diagnosed with an illness is a challenge but not always a catastrophe. Making a job or career change is a challenge. Receiving a political nomination also poses a challenge. However, situations such as these and many others often trigger a turning point for the better in a person's life.

With a little time and practice you're sure to devise your own guidelines.

KEY POINTS FOR READING TAROT CARDS IN ANY SPREAD

Major Arcana Cards 1-10[1] represents something you have earned through your recent behavior and actions.

Major Arcana Cards 11-22[2] tend to have a greater impact upon your long-range goals, and destiny.

Minor Arcana Cards 2-10 can signify situations, advantages, opportunities, moods or obstacles that come out of nowhere, and sometimes pass just as quickly.

Whenever a King appears, from any suit: Whatever your gender, your initiative is about to receive a boost – whether to set new wheels in motion or resolve an ongoing situation.

Whenever a Queen appears, from any suit: Whatever your gender or situation, your people and coping skills are about to be tested or required.

Whenever a Knight appears, from any suit: Whatever your gender, a Knights will inspire you to either reformulate your strategy or take a matter to the next level, in keeping with their suit.

Whenever a Page appears, from any suit: Even the smallest matters now have the potential to become better than you expected or more than you bargained for – a work in progress.

Whenever an Ace appears, from any suit: An inevitable showdown is approaching, whether with yourself, matters or other people. Aces are the Tarot's way of measuring your personal growth.

---

[1] Major Arcana Cards 1-10, are the Magician through Fortunes Wheel.
[2] Major Arcana Cards 11-22, are Justice through the Fool.

Whenever a Two appears, from any suit: the Seekers level of attachment to someone (or something) is about to increase or decrease.

Whenever a Three appears, from any suit: How the Seeker will absorb and react to whatever is happening around them will pertain to their mood.

Whenever a Four appears, from any suit: The Seekers sense of belonging or desire for security will have a stronger bearing upon matters now.

Whenever a Five appears, from any suit: The Seekers desire to suit themselves and still do the "right thing" in matters can pit their emotions against their logic.

Whenever a Six appears, from any suit: The Seekers willingness, to make whatever repairs may be necessary to keep matters running more smoothly, and efficiently–will be tested.

Whenever a Seven appears, from any suit: The constructive or self-destructive manner in which the Seeker is handling one or more of their relationships will become more apparent.

Whenever an Eight appears, from any suit: The Seeker will become more aware of opportunities and situations that have, or could potentially change their life.

Whenever a Nine appears, from any suit: Whether by choice or necessity the Seeker can broaden their horizons. "When you change the way you look at things, the things you look at change."

Whenever a Ten appears, from any suit: It's time for a realistic review (or reality check) of what the Seeker has achieved and hopes to achieve.

CHAPTER 10

TAROT DYNAMICS & THE MOON IN ASTROLOGY

TAROT DYNAMICS & THE HOROSCOPE SPREAD

You can do this spread anytime you wish but when you do, take notes. You'll be amazed at how accurately your Tarot Cards outline the prognosis of the coming months – especially if you treat yourself – or someone else to this reading for a birthday or at the start of the New Year! After you relax and shuffle your cards feel free to arrange the cards in any pattern you wish! If, (for example) your birthday falls in July you can choose whether to begin your reading by allowing Card Number One to represent July or August. If you have a question in October about next March you can choose whether to begin your reading by allowing Card Number One to represent October or November.

January	February	March	April
1	2	3	4

May	June	July	August
5	6	7	8

September	October	November	December
9	10	11	12

Before you retrieve each card's definition, take a moment to study the cards, and see what "feelings" you receive from the cards you selected.

MAJOR ARCANA CARDS = Personal Transformation. This month you'll be doing some soul-searching.

WANDS = Change. Wands blaze their own trail and this portends an adventurous or busy month ahead.

CUPS = Emotion. An emotional month at home, work or both that could improve your communication and understanding with yourself and other people too.

SWORDS = Challenge. Self-control is the key to transforming any challenges or delays that you encounter this month into an opportunity to succeed.

PENTACLES = Ambition. A good month for prioritizing, making and finalizing plans as well as setting yourself and matters in order.

TAROT DYNAMICS & THE MOON IN ASTROLOGY

At the onset of each New ●, Full ○, and First ☾ or Last Quarter Moon[1] ☽, even people who don't practice Astrology often become curious as to what might be in store for them, according to the upcoming Moon. In fact, many Tarot practitioners conduct a standard one or three card Tarot reading of their own, to see what lies ahead. While shuffling, cutting and drawing several of your own Tarot cards to see what each New, Full or Quarter Moon *may* bring you can be fun, what if we could use our Tarot Cards to be more specific? Well, now we can. Let's begin with a quick demonstration that will enable you to see how effective this simple process can be.

On November 16, 1963 there was a New Moon ● at 23° Scorpio ♏ 11 minutes[2]. Six days later on November 22, 1963 President John F. Kennedy was assassinated. According to our Lunar/Tarot Tables in 23° Scorpio ♏ corresponds to Card 47 the Seven of Cups. So everyone, everywhere in the world could expect to receive some type of opportunity, setback or simply enter a new phase of personal awareness in their affairs, directly or indirectly associated with the Seven of Cups. In Chapter 4, concerning Card 47 Tarot Dynamics says *"You're about to discover that you've over or underestimated someone - or something, for better or worse"*.

However, President Kennedy chose to ignore the misgivings about his trip to Dallas from his advisors – as well as

---

[1] Like many people, I too believe that the Crescent, Gibbous, Disseminating and Balsamic Moon Phases have a greater psychological than circumstantial impact.

[2] Remember, no matter where in the world you live, each New, Full and Quarter Moon occupies the same Sign at virtually the same degrees, even though it may not arrive on the same day.

Jeanne Dixon[3]. Let's pretend that President Kennedy had been proficient in the Tarot[4]. Perhaps after removing Card 47 from his deck and reviewing his most comfortable definition for Card 47, he might also have used it as a one card spread – to assist him in meditating upon that New Moon.

---

[3] World-renowned psychic astrologer now deceased.
[4] President Kennedy was not in any way connected with Tarot. This scenario is purely hypothetical.

Then again, he might have elected to conduct a two card spread such as this:

Card 1: The Seven of Cups, represents the Seeker as well As the General or Tone the of the New Moon

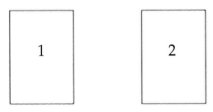

Card 2 (Draw one more card at random from your deck) Is This New Moon Likely To Help or Hinder My Progress?

Or Perhaps a three-card spread such as this could have shed even more light on matters:

Card 1 Seven of Cups Seeker's Tone of New Moon	Card 2 (Any Card) What I Stand To Learn From This New Moon	Card 3 (Any Card) What More Do I Need To Know?
1	2	3

Why not take a moment to think of what Tarot spreads you might devise using one Tarot card to serve as a signature or significator card for any or each New, Full or Quarter Moon. Consider too, how much easier and more accurate it will be to plan ahead and minimize (if not avoid) any number of minor or major mix-ups and misunderstandings with other people, that can and often do undermine even the sunniest personal readings – leaving you to say, "well I suppose it just wasn't meant to be".

For instance: You've scheduled several important talks or meetings for next week. Upon discovering there will also be a New, Full or Quarter Moon governed by Card 59 the Five of Swords, you immediately conduct a mini-reading, featuring Card 59 as the signature card (or significator) and thank goodness! The accompanying card(s) that represent your venture appear more positive. However, in Chapter 5, concerning Card 59 Tarot Dynamics says, *"Beware of overstepping your boundaries now in matters, at home, at work or both"*. Although you don't know the type of impact next weeks Moon will have on the people you're meeting with, you *do* know that Card 59 could present *them* with a few extra challenges. Best of all, you now know that by taking your cue from other people's moods and behavior you can "avoid overstepping your bounds" next week, and bring your concerns to the more successful conclusion that is being forecast by your other Tarot Cards.

Now let's see more of "what" this simple process can do, and "how" you can to apply it more effectively!

The late Princess Diana (a Cancer ♋ Sun-Sign) married Prince Charles (a Scorpio ♏ Sun-Sign) on July 29, 1981. It's a matter of public record now, that virtually up until they said, "I do" both Prince Charles and Princess Diana harbored serious misgivings concerning the success of their marriage. On July 24, 1981 (five days before their wedding) there was a third Quarter Moon ☐ at 1° Taurus[5] ♉. When you read our Lunar Factoids you'll learn that

---

[5] Technically the Moon came in at 1°24 minutes of Taurus. From: Michelsens American Ephemeris for the 20th Century. For our purposes however, only the degrees are necessary.

Taurus is one of four signs that trigger a personal reality check, concerning our long-range security and goals, and that " Last (or third) Quarter Moons are a time when you can clearly see what will and will not work for you."

From our Lunar/Tarot Tables in under the heading, Pentacles we see that:

Moon at 0°-10° Taurus = Card 73 the Five of Pentacles. In Chapter 6 concerning the Five of Pentacles, Tarot Dynamics says: *"One or two matters are either not going to go your way or move as smoothly as you had hoped"*. As that third quarter Moon only echoed her concerns it was not a particularly auspicious indication. We can only speculate what other cards the Prince or Princess might have drawn to accompany Card 73. Two days after their wedding On July 31, 1981 there was a New Moon ● Eclipse at 7° Leo ♌. Leo is a sign that also triggers some degree of activity, interest or concern about our long-range security and goals. New Moons can equal New Starts – a time to formulate new plans and set new goals, since this New Moon was also an eclipse, it would pack some additional "punch."

From our Lunar/Tarot Tables under the heading entitled Wands we find: Moon at 0°-10° Leo = Card 31 the Five of Wands.

In Chapter 3, concerning the Five of Wands, Tarot Dynamics says: "Unexpected events at work and at home could cause you to question yourself, your work, goals or the sincerity of people around you. Here, the Wand's desire to blaze their own trail, becomes your trial by fire." So we can only imagine what other cards the Princess (or Prince) might have drawn to accompany the Five of Wands. From one biographer after another, we know now that neither the Prince nor Princess had the honeymoon of their dreams.

Although the wedding and honeymoon for the Prince and (late) Princess of Wales provided numerous hints of the misfortunes yet to come, let's also remember that theirs was a unique situation. Just like any other reading, when a Moon is governed by a Subject Card it can also indicate no more than a "tempest in a teapot" that could blow in and over very quickly. Had they been more secure as a couple, although Card 73 the Five of Pentacles did precede their wedding those "one or two matters that are not going to go as smoothly as you hoped", might have related to the issues concerning the train on Diana's' gown or the moment she mistook Charles's second name for his third. Had they been more comfortable with one another the appearance of Card 31 the Five of Wands for their honeymoon might have served as the catalyst that led to an open discussion that could have cleared the air, concerning those cufflinks from Camilla and the photo of her the Prince was keeping in one of his books.

Now let's use a world event for our next and most significant example. "It was on September 15, 2008 when Lehman Brothers collapsed and the Dow dropped 500-points that the panic surrounding the financial crisis peaked[6]" However, it was on Monday September 29, 2008[7] when the Dow fell 778 points in the biggest single-day loss to date, and paved the way to the ultimate crash on October 6, 2008. On September 29, 2008 there was a New Moon ● at 6° Libra[8] ♎ Astrologers consider Aries♈, Cancer♋, Libra♎ and Capricorn♑ to be the biggest "movers and shakers" in the zodiac. So whenever a New, Full or Quarter Moon, AND it's retainer changes into one of these four

---

[6] From Mint.com on September 24, 2010

[7] From money.cnn.com September 29, 2008 and Money-Zine.com "Stock Market Crash of 2008."

[8] Technically the Moon came in at 6°33 minutes of Libra. From: Michelsens American Ephemeris for the 21st Century, 2001 -2050 Midnight.

signs, no matter what your sun-sign, they can get matters moving, energize or upset your agenda and behavior in ways and at times when you least expect it."

Unlike the Moon changes in our earlier examples, since this New Moon is being governed by a Court Card and it's retainer[9] whatever events accompany it and whatever personal actions the Seeker will initiate or repress are likely to have a more immediate, definite or longer-lasting effect upon them, and their goals.

Any Moon at 0°–10° Libra = Card 51 the King of Swords + Card 56 the Two of Swords.

In our Lunar-Tarot Guide under the heading, Swords you will learn that:

" Although this Moon Change can heighten your determination and ability to maintain your emotional and material goals, should you be overstressed it can also handicap your desire or ability to handle matters more effectively, and lead you to become more dependent upon other people – or simply more vulnerable to deception from the wrong people".

From Chapter 5, concerning Card 51 the King of Swords, Tarot Dynamics says: "The more challenging the situation or other cards in the spread the more likely you are to blame other people for your lack of focus and preparation". Concerning Card 56 the Two of Swords, Tarot Dynamics also says: "There is some uncertainty about a matter at work, at home, or both. Whatever your situation, the Two of Swords can enable you to develop a more reliable method to help you cope – whether with situations you can't change, losses you can't prevent or people that you can't seem to please".

---

[9] From Chapter 15 the Lunar Mini-Guide "each King in the Minor Arcana can rely upon the Two from his suit to reinforce his initiative, and yours too!

Yes, under that New Moon the stock market did indeed collapse, due to matters that had grown beyond anyone's ability to control or contain them any longer – unleashing a tsunami of events that everyone in the world is still grappling with in one way or another, three years later! Yet, however accurate this was it was not only an extreme, but also an extremely rare example of the potential that can be unleashed by any and every New, Full or Quarter Moon governed by Aries, Cancer, Libra or Capricorn[10].

On the next page we'll begin a final demonstration featuring the aver- age person dealing with a New Moon at 6° Libra. For instance: You're a long-time employee, with an immaculate work record and you've been waiting for the "best time" to approach your boss about a raise in pay. Your speech is prepared, you're feeling confident and since New Moons equal New Starts you feel there's no time like the present.

---

[10] To date, the only other example would the bombing of the London Subway on July 7, 2005, which was preceded by a New Moon ☽ at 14° Cancer ♋ on July 6, 2005. Americas entry in WW II on December 7, 1941 was preceded by a Full Moon ☽ at 11° Gemini♊ on December 3, 1941 (card 60 the Six of Swords). The official beginning of the Great Depression, which began on October 29, 1929 was preceded by a Third Quarter Moon ☽ at 1° Leo ♌on October 25, 1929 (Card 31 the Five of Wands)

Moon at 0°–10° Libra = Card 51 the King of Swords + Card 56 the Two of Swords.

Signature Card 1: The King of Swords Represents.

The Seeker and General Tone of the New Moon

Signature Card 2: The Two of Swords

Represents factors or events that can clarify or complicate matters this week.

Now let's see how these two cards can help you prepare or plan ahead more easily.

Card 1: The King of Swords   Keywords: Challenging/Initiative

Clearly this New Moon ☐ will set a more "challenging" tone or mood for everyone. Yet the term "challenging" does not mean that your request will not be granted. It can simply imply a busier, or more active tone and mood. Since your boss is likely to have other matters on his mind, it may be a bit more "challenging" for you to choose the right moment to obtain his undivided attention, even though the suit of Swords is synonymous with communication.

From Chapter 5, concerning Card 51 the King of Swords Tarot Dynamics says:

Since you are likely to be more outspoken now, it may be easier than usual for you to relate to other people who are the same way.

Card 2: The Two of Swords   Keywords: Challenging/
Attachments

In Chapter 5, concerning Card 56 the Two of Swords Tarot Dynamics also says:

With the Two of Swords personal determination can be your perfect companion or your worst enemy. There is some uncertainty about a matter at work, at home, or both. You may be waiting for an answer, formulating a reply or preparing to initiate a request or discussion. On the following page, Tarot Dynamics says:

"Despite its fondness for company like the 2nd House in Astrology, our 2's also signal an element of concern about how much we feel we're receiving in return, from other people and matters.

While each of these statements reinforces the significance of choosing the right moment to approach your boss, the second statement also implies the possibility that you may also find it more "challenging" than you expected not to back down.

The more confidence you have in you as well as your relationship with your boss, the more likely you can obtain your goal, simply by following these initial guidelines. However, what if, despite your long-time service and great work record you barely know your boss? Obtaining this raise is important to you, and you don't wish to make a mistake. Since The Two of Swords also says: "the more encouraging the situation or other cards in the spread, the easier you can play the "waiting-game" in matters now. Any delays you encounter now are more likely to work in your favor strengthening your position as well as your resolve". So, before you decide whether to forge ahead or back down, perhaps you might consider drawing one more card to assist you.

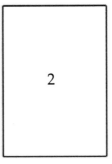

Signature Card 1: The King of Swords Represents:

The Seeker and the General Tone the New Moon

Signature Card 2: The Two of Swords Represents:

Factors which could clarify or complicate matters this week.

Card 3: (Whatever Card You Draw At Random From Your Deck)

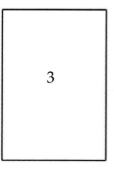

Card 3: Represents What Else You Need To Know

So the next time that you consult your ephemeris or your favorite Astrology Web Site to view the Astrological sign and degrees of the upcoming New, Full or Quarter Moon, don't forget to consult your Tarot Dynamics Moon Phase Tables to see what more you might discover!

POINTS TO CONSIDER

Though similar to the way that Astrologers make their monthly and weekly forecasts, this process can enable us, as Tarot practitioners, to broaden our intuitive, psychological and circumstantial horizons as we quickly and easily become more familiar with our Tarot cards.

Should you wish to discover more about determining your most favorable cycles to assist you in choosing the best times to take action and promote your endeavors, you might simply study the Tarot Card that represents each New, Full or Quarter Moon, and take notes concerning your activities during that week – paying special attention to whether matters (and your moods) seem to remain the same, improve, or become more complex. This exercise could assist you in discovering which Tarot cards are most compatible with your personal rhythm, and how to handle more frustrating times with greater efficiency.

Since it's not unusual for certain Tarot Cards (especially, among the "mover and shaker" category) to repeat themselves once or sometimes even twice a year, discovering which single cards as well as combinations, work best for you, could enable you to plan ahead more smoothly.

QUICK & EASY LUNAR FACTOIDS

Astrologically:

Each New ●, Full ○ or Quarter Moon ☽ introduces some type of opportunity, set-back or new level of personal awareness, which makes it easier or more challenging to keep pace with current matters , while striving to reach other goals.

While An Eclipse is nothing more than a New or Full Moon – that packs some additional punch....

New Moons ● are believed to equal New Starts, a time when anything is possible – a work in progress. Although New Moons are a good time to launch well-planned matters, they're also a time when, other matters can take us by surprise-for better or worse. So because New Moons are a time when wishes that we've made, as well as those we make are more likely to be granted or denied, our key phrase for New Moons is:

"I Wish"

Full Moons ○   are synonymous with releasing or letting go of tension, so they tend to be associated with concluding matters- much like the end of a chapter. Yet because they can also remove obstacles that have been blocking our path, so that we may launch other projects more smoothly, our Full Moon key-phrase is:

"Matters I can now complete or set aside"

As there are *approximately* two weeks between each New and Full Moon, there's a common (yet understandable) misconception that the full-force of the New or Full Moon energy sets the pace for the entire two weeks – but they don't. *Approximately* seven days after each New Moon there is a First Quarter Moon, and *approximately* seven days after each Full Moon there is a Last (or third) Quarter Moon. Like the intermission at a concert or a play, Quarter

Moons enable us to decide whether to stay for the entire performance or leave early – whether to return home or pursue a more appealing prospect.

First Quarter Moons ☽ inspire you to begin taking action-whether by taking the helm in matter after matter to save the day, or start the ball rolling. So whether you're dancing with delight or frustration, since your energy and inspiration are less likely to be wasted our key phrase for First Quarter Moons is:
"I can do"

Last (or third) Quarter Moons ☽ are a time when you can clearly see what will and will not work for you – enabling you to make any necessary adjustments, or realize that changing your present course is not in your best interest – at least for now. So because Last Quarter Moons can enable us to see the "bigger picture" more clearly in matters, our key phrase for Last Quarter Moons is:
"I have learned"

ASTROLOGICALLY:

Collectively, Astrologers, consider Aries ♈, Cancer ♋, Libra ♎ and Capricorn ♑[11] to be the biggest "movers and shakers" in the zodiac, due to their correlation with the four points on the compass. So no matter what your sun sign[12], during the four months[13] out of every year (along with any Quarter Moons) governed by these signs, the Court Cards and their retainers[14] can get matters moving, energize or upset your agenda and behavior in ways, and at times when you least expect it – just like Card 1 the Magician, and every number 4, 7, and 10 card from each suit in the Tarot, all of whom correlate to Houses 1, 4, 7 and 10, which are governed by Aries, Cancer, Libra and Capricorn.

Collectively, Taurus ♉, Leo ♌, Scorpio ♏ and Aquarius ♒[15] symbolize your long-range goals for security and stability. Whenever a New, Full or Quarter Moon, is governed by of these four signs [16], no matter what your Sun-Sign, you're likely to experience some additional activity, interest, or concern about the future of your security and long-range goals. Although these signs can trigger a personal "reality check" that can keep your and other people "on the same page" and matters on target, if you've been taking to much for granted or to personally, you may also be to slow to make adjustments or too quick to make mountains out of molehills – just like every number 2, 5, and 8 card from each suit in the Tarot,

---

[11] Aries, Cancer, Libra and Capricorn are the Cardinal Signs in Astrology.
[12] Although they can have a stronger impact upon people born under the sign of Aries, Cancer, Libra or Capricorn.
[13] Aries: March 21-April 20. Cancer: June 22 -July 22. Libra: September 23 – Oct. 23. Capricorn: December 22 – January 20.
[14] Chapter 2 introduced you to the old-time Tarot Kingdoms and the Court Cards retainers. For example, the Two from each suit serves it's King, while the Three serves the Queen and the Four serves the Page in the Minor Arcana.
[15] Taurus, Leo, Scorpio and Aquarius are the Fixed Signs in Astrology.
[16] Although they can have a stronger impact upon people born under the sign of Taurus, Leo, Scorpio or Aquarius.

whom also correspond to Houses 2, 5 and 8, which are governed by Taurus, Leo and Scorpio.

Collectively, Gemini ♊, Virgo ♍, Sagittarius ♐ and Pisces ♓[17] often test, reward and strengthen your adaptability – sometimes by pointing out your vulnerability. So whenever any New, Full or Quarter Moons, are governed by one of these four signs[18], no matter what your Sun-Sign, you could launch an endeavor more smoothly, see matters more clearly or let go of a non-productive issue more easily. Then again, if you've been too sure of yourself, or too quick to "leap before you look" you could become too deflated by matters or people that fail to meet your expectations – just like every number 3, 6, and 9 card from each suit in the Tarot, all of whom correlate to Houses 3, 6 and 9, which are governed by Gemini, Virgo and Sagittarius.

---

[17] Gemini, Virgo, Sagittarius & Pisces are the Mutable Signs in Astrology.
[18] Although they can have a stronger impact upon people born under the sign of Gemini, Virgo, Sagittarius or Pisces.

YOUR LUNAR TAROT-GUIDE

Since Aries ♈, Cancer ♋, Libra ♎ and Capricorn ♑ to be the biggest "movers and shakers" in the zodiac, no matter what your sun sign, anytime a New, Full, First or Last Quarter Moon is being governed by one of these signs you always give or receive a little more than you expected. Since these are the ONLY signs governed by a Court card and the retainer that matches their suit, these Moons can get matters moving, energize or even upset your agenda in ways, and at times when you least expect it. So whether or not your week is twice as busy, the news or matters that unfold then often prove to be twice as important.

Each King, in the Minor Arcana can rely upon the Two from his suit to reinforce his initiative, and yours too!

Each Queen, in the Minor Arcana can rely upon the Three from her suit to enhance her charm, and sharpen her people and networking skills, and so can you!

Each Page, in the Minor Arcana can rely upon the Four from their Suit to enhance their element of surprise and alternate between keeping them focused and amused, and you can too!

WANDS

The King, Queen and Page of Wands and each of their retainers represent the Sign of Aries.

In terms of personal initiative because Card 28 the Two of Wands is second only to Card 23 the King of Wands, so whenever they appear together, they can be one of the most self-constructive or self-destructive card combinations.

Since an Aries Moon tends to make you more aware of the impact that whatever you're doing or whoever you're with is having on you, those governed by the King and Two of Wands also lend you the energy to bring yourself and matters under better control – unless it seems matters are running away with you, in which case, you'd be wise to watch your temper and be on guard against miscalculations or impulsive behavior that could trigger an unpleasant disagreement or accident[19].

When it comes to choosing the right time, opportunity and people, the Three of Wands is second only to the Queen of Wands. So, anytime they're together, they can form one of the most vivacious or vicious Tarot combinations.

When an Aries Moon is being governed by the Queen and Three of Wands since it tends to stimulate your desire for adventure, attention, advancement, or even romance, it can also activate your ability to create or act more quickly upon any opportunities to reach your goals. Should you be overstressed however, you may also take unfair advantage of matters, or take too many matters the wrong way[20].

---

[19] Mini-Astrological correlation, the 1st House and Mars
[20] Mini-Astrological correlation the 5th House and the Sun

As far as organization and timing the Four of Wands is second only to the Page of Wands, which can render their influence uncommonly straightforward, intelligent and well-organized or completely haphazard.

When an Aries Moon is being governed by the Page and Four of Wands it can be a time of discovery or revelation that can replenish or diminish your faith and optimism. Sometimes they can even change your luck –even if they only accompany situations designed to help you learn from your mistakes before you repeat them[21].

---

[21] Mini-Astrological correlation the 9th House and Jupiter

CUPS

The King, Queen and Page of Cups as well as their retainers represent the Sign of Cancer.

In terms of emotional initiative, since Card 42 the Two of Cups is second only to Card 37 the King of Cups, any time they're together, they can prove to be incredibly compelling and endearing or conniving – and somewhat controlling.

Moons governed by Cancer tend to increase your satisfaction or dissatisfaction with your place and role in life. With the King and Two of Cups, the happier you are the stronger your desire and ability to impress, improve, or (if necessary) defend whatever or whoever you feel to be yours. However, should you be overstressed, or feeling overwhelmed by matters– you may also feel moody, or secretive and mistrustful[22].

---

[22] Mini-Astrological correlation, the 4th House and the Moon

When it comes to fact finding, the Three of Cups is second only to the Queen of Cups. Since neither of them is ever without an agenda when acquiring or delivering information they can exert a particularly sensitive and intelligent or deliberately inconsiderate and tactless influence.

Since Moons governed by the Queen and Three of Cups tend to heighten your concern and interest, in your future you'll sometimes find it easier to initiate situations that will improve matters or allow you greater control. However, the greater your frustration with matters, anyone or anything, the easier confusion could weaken your self-control and better judgment, leading you to deliberately misinterpret or simply avoid dealing with situations that make you uncomfortable[23].

---

[23] Mini-Astrological correlation the 8th House and Pluto

Concerning sound material and emotional organization, the Four of Cups is second only to the Page of Cups, which can make them two of the most focused and perceptive, or naïve and inconsistent combinations in the Tarot.

Although Moons governed by the Page and Four of Cups can take the edge off tense situations by enabling you to view matters more realistically, or sharpening your intuition and creativity – should you be overstressed they can also lull you into a false sense of security or generate a what's-the-use-attitude, that can temporarily undermine your resolve or progress[24].

---

[24] Mini-Astrological correlation the 12th House and Neptune

SWORDS

The King, Queen and Page of Swords, as well as each of their retainers represent the Sign of Libra.

As far as mental and psychological agility and initiative, the Two of Swords is second only to the King of Swords, so whenever they get together, they can exert a particularly efficient and inspirational, or confusing and distracting influence.

Although Moons governed by Libra tend to intensify your ability to maintain and improve your social or emotional status quo, they can also accentuate the best and worst features in our personalities and relationships. So should you be overstressed, those governed by the King and Two of Swords can sometimes handicap your ability to handle matters more effectively, which can lead you to become

 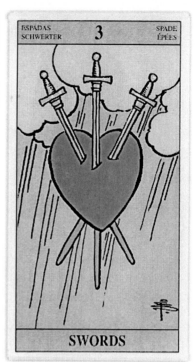

more dependent upon other people – or more vulnerable to deception from the wrong people[25].

As far as mental and psychological understanding, the Three of Swords is second only to the Queen of Swords, and whenever they get together, they can be one of the most universally enlightened or personally embattled combinations in the Tarot.

So although Moons that fall under their influence, can increase your capability for reaching a personal goal, mending fences or even uniting other people should you be overstressed your patience and diplomacy may both be in short supply when dealing with unexpected inter-ruptions or sresistance[26].

---

[25] Mini-Astrological correlation the 7th House and Venus
[26] Mini-Astrological correlation the 11th House and Uranus

In terms of mental versatility and agility, the Four of Swords is second only to the Page of Swords, which makes them one of the most organized and patient or unfortunately impulsive combinations in the Tarot.

When Moons governed by the Page and Four of Swords enable you to see both sides of matters more clearly, they can also lend you better control of your responses and reactions. However, should you be overstressed, the tendency to do too much in some instances and too little in others can create additional con- fusion and anxiety that will take even longer to resolve[27].

---

[27] Mini-Astrological correlation the 3rd House and Mercury

PENTACLES

The King, Queen and Page of Pentacles, as well as each of their retainers, represent the Sign of Capricorn.

In terms of practical accord and initiative, since the Two of Pentacles is second only to the King of Pentacles whenever they appear together, they can be one of the most shrewd, dependable and self-disciplined or self- involved ,undependable and irresponsible combinations in the Tarot.

Although Moons governed by Capricorn can assist you in recognizing, accepting and meeting your responsibilities more easily and realistically, should you be overstressed when the King and Two of Pentacles are in charge, everything you're doing may feel less enjoyable[28].

---

[28] Mini-Astrological correlation the 10th House and Saturn

When it comes to practical achievement, the Three of Pentacles is second only to the Queen of Pentacles, which can enable them to be one of the most ambitious, persistent and creative, or selfish, meddlesome, and stubborn combinations in the Tarot.

Although each Moon governed by the Queen and Three of Pentacles has the potential to bring material as well as emotional harmony and attraction into matters, should you be overstressed, harmony can quickly become disharmony and matters or people that recently appeared so attractive can bore or irritate you no end [29].

---

[29] Mini-Astrological correlation the 2nd House and Venus

In terms of practical accord and initiative, since the Four of Pentacles is second only to the Page of Pentacles whenever they appear together, they can be one of the most thoughtful and well-prepared or depressive and indecisive combinations in the Tarot.

Although any Moon that falls under the influence of the Page and Four of Pentacles can boost your organizational abilities – should you be overstressed they can also lead you to change your mind unexpectedly or resurrect issues, fears or grievances from the past that you thought had been resolved[30].

---

[30] Mini-Astrological correlation the 6th House and Mercury

YOUR LUNAR/TAROT TABLES

By slightly amending[31] the synthesis[32] for combining Astrology and the Tarot put forth by Faith Javane and Dusty Bunker from Pages 260 – 263 in their book "Numerology and the Divine Triangle" we can now use our Tarot Cards to gain more practical insight about what's in store for us under each New, Full, First or Last Quarter Moon. For your convenience only the Court Cards and their Retainer are in bold print.

WANDS

Card 23 King of Wands	**Moon at 0°–10°Aries**
Card 24 Queen of Wands	**Moon at 11°–20° Aries**
Card 26 Page of Wands	**Moon at 21°–30°Aries**
Card 28 Two of Wands	**Moon at 0°–10°Aries**
Card 29 Three of Wands	**Moon at 11°–20° Aries**
Card 30 Four of Wands	**Moon at 21°–30°Aries**
Card 31 Five of Wands	Moon at 0°–10° Leo
Card 32 Six of Wands	Moon at 11°–20° Leo
Card 33 Seven of Wands	Moon at 21°–30° Leo

---

[31] As this is a Tarot Book, I chose not to include Ms. Javane and Bunkers planetary rulers and Tarot Dynamics translated the decans into the Tarot Cards.
[32] Although there are any number of combinations for blending Astrology and the Tarot, the one that I have found to be the most reliable was put forth by Faith Javane and Dusty Bunker on Page 264 of their book "Numerology and the Divine Triangle." Much like any other synthesis, according to the ladies Javane and Bunker all twenty-two cards, from the Major Arcana are governed by certain planets and combinations of planets and, while each Knight (or defender of the realm) from the Minor Arcana, governs one particular season (Spring, Summer, Fall and Winter) every Ace in the Minor Arcana represents one of the four elements (Fire, Earth, Air and Water) or kingdom in which each suit resides. You may refer back to Chapter 2 for additional clarification. However, the remaining forty-eight Minor Arcana cards are ideal for our purpose.

Card 34 Eight of Wands   Moon at 0°–10° Sagittarius

Card 35 Nine of Wands   Moon at 11°–20° Sagittarius

Card 36 Ten of Wands   Moon at 21°–30° Sagittarius

CUPS

Card 37 **King of Cups**   **Moon at 0°–10° Cancer**

Card 38 **Queen of Cups**   **Moon at 11°–20° Cancer**

Card 40 **Page of Cups**   **Moon at 21°–30° Cancer**

Card 42 **Two of Cups**   **Moon at 0°–10° Cancer**

Card 43 **Three of Cups**   **Moon at 11°–20° Cancer**

Card 44 **Four of Cups**   **Moon at 21°–30° Cancer**

Card 45 Five of Cups   Moon at 0°–10° Scorpio

Card 46 Six of Cups   Moon at 11°–20° Scorpio

Card 47 Seven of Cups   Moon at 21°–30° Scorpio

Card 48 Eight of Cups   Moon at 0°–10° Pisces

Card 49 Nine of Cups   Moon at 11°–20° Pisces

Card 50 Ten of Cups   Moon at 21°–30° Pisces

SWORDS

Card 51 **King of Swords**   **Moon at 0°–10° Libra**

Card 52 **Queen of Swords**   **Moon at 11°–20° Libra**

Card 54 **Page of Swords**   **Moon at 21°–30° Libra**

Card 56 **Two of Swords**   **Moon at 0°–10° Libra**

Card 57 **Three of Swords**   **Moon at 11°–20° Libra**

Card 58 **Four of Swords**   **Moon at 21°–30° Libra**

Card 59 Five of Swords   Moon at 0°–10° Aquarius

Card 60 Six of Swords   Moon at 11°–20° Aquarius

Card 61 Seven of Swords	Moon at 21°–30° Aquarius
Card 62 Eight of Swords	Moon at 0°–10° Gemini
Card 63 Nine of Swords	Moon at 11°–20° Gemini
Card 64 Ten of Swords	Moon at 21°–30° Gemini

PENTACLES

Card 65 King of Pentacles	**Moon at 0°–10° Capricorn**
Card 66 Queen of Pentacles	**Moon at 11°–20° Capricorn**
Card 68 Page of Pentacles	**Moon at 21°–30° Capricorn**
Card 70 Two of Pentacles	**Moon at 0°–10° Capricorn**
Card 71 Three of Pentacles	**Moon at 11°–20° Capricorn**
Card 72 Four of Pentacles	**Moon at 21°–30° Capricorn**
Card 73 Five of Pentacles	Moon at 0°–10° Taurus
Card 74 Six of Pentacles	Moon at 11°–20° Taurus
Card 75 Seven of Pentacles	Moon at 21°–30° Taurus
Card 76 Eight of Pentacles	Moon at 0°-10° Virgo
Card 77 Nine of Pentacles	Moon at 11°-20° Virgo
Card 78 Ten of Pentacles	Moon at 21°-30° Virgo

NOTE: Although these tables are an effective means for delivering a more accurate weekly forecast with your Tarot Cards, as well as minor planetary interpretations, more significant research will be required before they can be recognized or considered a reliable method for Natal, Transit or Progressed Chart interpretation.

Anna Burroughs Cook, author of "Tarot Dynamics" and Tarot Dynamics Unleashed" has been teaching and reading the Tarot for 30+ years, for clients across the United States and Great Britain, as well as in Ohio, where she currently resides with her hubby, Rick (who gave Tarot Dynamics it's name) as well as Suzy Q their Spoiled Rottenweiler, Cagney, their "Good" Shepherd, and Buddy, their Super-Spaniel!

Where To Connect With Anna:

Tarot Dynamics
www.tarotdynamics.com
Tarot Dynamics Group on Face Book
tarotdynamics@groups.facebook.com

If you enjoyed this book (and naturally we hope that you did) we recommend the following titles for your further reading enjoyment.

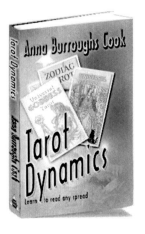

Tarot Dynamics – Learn to Read any spread also by Anna Burroughs Cook is a companion book to Tarot Dynamics Unleashed and offers sage advice and the insightful revelations into the interpretation of your favorite tarot deck. Literally any deck may be used without difficulty.

ISBN: 978-0-9814278-1-2

The DeepTeachings of Merlyn by Douglas Monroe, is the third in the Merlyn Trilogy, and covers Druidic Magic based on the early Book of Pherylt. It is also a charmingly written story of the induction of the young and future King Arthur as an apprentice Druid and Magician.

The book also includes extensive modern research into the science of inter-dimensional travel and other world realities.

ISBN: 978-1-920533-16-9 Trade Paper, 978-1-920535-15-5 eBook

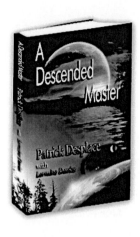

A Descended Master by Patrick Desplace with Lorraine Davies is a masterful work on magic and sorcery by a Master Occultist and esotericist.

This unique exploration of consciousness is an exceptionally valuable offering to the world. It is at the cutting edge of perception and totally relevant to the challenges of today's world

ISBN: 978-1-920535-11-7 Trade Paper, 978-1-920535-16-2 eBook

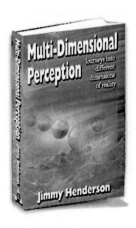

Multi-Dimensional Perception – Journeys into Different Dimensions of reality by Jimmy Henderson is another angle to gaining full awakening which includes some advanced processes and guidelines to working with energy. The book is infused with Rosicrucian wisdom.

ISBN: 978-0-9814278-8-1 Trade Paper 978 -0-9869858-1-2 eBook

Visit us for many more exciting titles
http://www.kimaglobalbooks.com

Kima Global Publishers is an independent publishing house based in Cape Town South Africa, but globally based. Our books are available throughout the English speaking world.

We offer an unique variety of titles in a wide range of Mind, Body and Spirit genres, including: alternative healing, wellness, spiritual philosophy, parenting, coaching, visionary and spiritual fiction and creative work books.

We invite you to visit:

www.kimaglobalbooks.com
for books or
www.kimaglobalpublishers.com
for author submissions.

Lightning Source UK Ltd.
Milton Keynes UK
UKOW04f2014170415

249872UK00001B/25/P